EQUINE

Portland Jones is a writer, horse trainer and lecturer who lives and works in Western Australia's Swan Valley. She has a PhD in Literature and her first novel was short-listed for the TAG Hungerford Award. Her second novel was short-listed for the richest genre-based literary award in Australasia, the ARA Historical Novel Prize.

As a horse trainer, Portland has a strong focus on welfare and teaches an evidence-based training strategy. She also teaches equine behaviour at Murdoch University.

Portland is also a trainer for The Help Foundation, a charity that works with captive populations of endangered Asian elephants to ensure their ongoing welfare.

A Love Letter to the Horse

PORTLAND JONES

First published 2026

Exisle Publishing Pty Ltd
C/o Shortland Chartered Accountants Ltd, Level 9, 51 Shortland Street,
Auckland 1010, New Zealand
PO Box 864, Chatswood, NSW 2057, Australia
www.exislepublishing.com

A CiP record for this book is available from the National Library of Australia.

ISBN 978-1-923011-08-3

Designed by Bee Creative
Typeset in PT Serif, 11pt
Printed by Lightning Source

This book uses paper sourced under ISO 14001 guidelines from well-managed forests and other controlled sources.

10 9 8 7 6 5 4 3 2 1

Disclaimer
While this book is intended as a general information resource and all care has been taken in compiling the contents, neither the author nor the publisher and their distributors can be held responsible for any loss, injury, claim or action that may arise from reliance on the information contained in this book.

To Carla Huisken

For teaching us that a goal worth having is worth working for.

CONTENTS

INTRODUCTION

'Men have forgotten this truth,' said the fox. 'But you must not forget it. You become responsible, for ever, for what you have tamed.'

–*Antoine de Saint Exupéry*

It is impossible to talk about the history of the horse without talking about the history of humanity, because for thousands of years humans and horses have lived, played and worked alongside each other. However, even the 6000 years of our coexistence cannot adequately explain the complex and nuanced relationship between our species. Horses don't just live amongst us; they live *within* us. They are embedded in our language, our culture and our psyche to an extraordinary degree and even today, in the 21st century, when very few people actually need a horse for work, the world's population of horses is still booming. And while mutual need may have driven the start of our relationship, it is our love for the horse that keeps us together.

I can't remember a time in my life when I didn't love horses. To me, they are the most beautiful of all the domesticated animals. I wasn't born into a horse-loving family, but I think the love of horses is like a recessive gene that may not be apparent for generations until it suddenly occurs, like a blue-eyed child born to brown-eyed parents. I think that my parents, like the parents of other horse-loving children, believed I would grow out of it, until I didn't. And then they gradually and gracefully habituated to the smell of horses and the trail of dirt, hay and horse hair that is the inevitable consequence of loving a horse.

I never thought of my childhood as unique or extraordinary, and it wasn't at the time, but it seems so now in the context of my own 21st-century parenting. It was almost entirely unsupervised and spent with friends on horses. We fell often (without helmets), rode for hours (without water bottles) and somehow managed to get home in time for dinner (without mobile phones). Luck has played a significant role in my life in many ways, not only because we all managed to escape serious injury but because I am so incredibly lucky to have spent a lot of my childhood in the most enjoyable classroom of all — outside and with animals.

I'm not sure when I began to understand that our relationship with the horse was not always in the horse's best interests, but from inside the horse industry it's not hard to see. Margins are tight, time is short and there are enormous pressures on those who choose to make their living from the horse. Also, tradition runs deep in the equestrian world and while engaging in practices that are centuries old may give us a sense of continuity and a connection to the past, cleaving to ancient practices for the sake of maintaining tradition is not only pointless, it can be destructive. Over the years the expression 'We do it this way because this is the way it has always been done' has been used as a justification for a lot of very questionable practices. Our understanding and knowledge of what constitutes good welfare has changed so much in the intervening centuries that sometimes sticking to the traditional ways makes as much sense as, for example, eschewing modern medicine and using bloodletting as the sole treatment for gout and epilepsy.

~

Just as I was beginning to understand that there must be a better way to train and manage the horse, luck intervened, yet again. My partner and I were given a very troubled horse. Ricky had been a successful racehorse, contesting over 50 races in his six-year career. Then, when he was no longer fast enough to be viable, he was bought by a showjumping rider who trained him to jump competitively. What began as a tendency to being unreliable and flighty turned, over time, into some fairly dangerous behaviour and eventually Ricky was sold to the rodeo to try out as a bucking horse. However, instead of bucking when the chute was opened, Ricky simply galloped in a terrified frenzy around the arena and this put an end to that career path.

Lucky for Ricky he was chocolate-box pretty. He was bright bay with a thin white stripe down his face and a graceful, arched neck. In those days, the bucking string of the rodeo was the last chance for difficult horses, a stay of execution that lasted as long as they kept bucking when the chute opened. And although Ricky didn't make it in the rodeo, his good looks earned him a reprieve from the death sentence that, sadly, is inevitable for many horses deemed too difficult.

When he arrived, Ricky was difficult to handle and extremely anxious. It seemed to me that his brain had retreated to a place where our actions and our attempted interactions were unable to reach him. Again, luck intervened. While reading an equestrian magazine I came across an article by Andrew McLean, a horse trainer in Victoria, Australia, who was conducting research into equine behaviour as part of his PhD thesis. I had then, and still have, my generation's faith in the power of science and it seemed to me that an empirical, evidence-based approach to horse training was long overdue. I wrote Andrew a letter and his reply, a few weeks later, began what has been a 25-year friendship that endures to this day.

In the 1990s, Andrew was at the forefront of a groundswell of scientific interest in the interactions between horses and humans. This interest eventually led to a new field of scientific endeavour, which has become known as equitation science. One of the fastest growing areas of scientific research, equitation science attempts to find evidence-based answers to age-old questions. By doing this, it doesn't seek to make mundane the relationship between our species, but rather it unravels the mysteries and opens the door to a world of knowledge that is at once more meaningful and far more extraordinary.

Equitation science allows us to make the best decisions about the horse's welfare because it offers objective ways to measure and assess it and, by providing a thorough understanding of the horse's behaviour and evolution, it allows us to determine the best practices for both training and management.

And equitation science comes just in time. The relationship between horses and humans is under pressure. Our world is changing rapidly and there is no part of it that escapes scrutiny. Human interactions with animals are more and more under the spotlight of the electronic media and that scrutiny has a way of changing our perspective. Today it seems abhorrent to kill an animal for its fur alone (and rightly so) when only 50 years ago very few people thought twice about it. In twenty years' time, if the way we interact with horses has not changed, what conclusions will people draw when they examine the relationship between horses and humans? Because right now equestrian is the most dangerous sport you can participate in (other than base jumping) and one in which we accept the wastage of its equine participants as inevitable.

~

Those of us who love and work with horses have inherited a tradition as old as any trade. And, just like our ancestors, we don't own the horse as a species; we simply hold it in trust for the generations yet to come. It is up to us to be the best and most ethical custodians of the horse and to future-proof the relationship between our species. If we want the children of our grandchildren to enjoy the horse as we do, we must ensure that one day, when the time comes, we can stand up to the critics of horse sports and say that we nurtured the horse even though it was not always easy. That we turned away from the ease of ancient beliefs and practices and embraced science so that we could train, manage and love the horse in ways that understand, embrace and celebrate the differences between our two species.

When I started to learn about the science of the horse I felt as if I was watching one of those magic shows that explains how the magician saws their lovely assistant in half (spoiler alert: they use a box with a false floor). In those shows, the reality of the illusion is so much more interesting and exciting than our assumptions. And that is true of the horse too. We have spent 6000 years telling ourselves stories about the horse and yet the science and the reality is far more fascinating and immeasurably more beautiful than the myth.

This book is a very small down payment on the huge debt of gratitude that I owe the horse. Horses have been my passion, my guide and my salvation. They have introduced me to lifelong friends, given me many memories of great joy and countless lessons in love. What I know about courage, patience and persistence I learned at the side of a horse. Horses keep me curious about the world and, even today, after many decades of life amongst them, they still fill me with awe.

As a horse trainer I have failed more often and made more mistakes than I'd ever like to count, but the horse is the most wonderful teacher. It is without question an enormous privilege to work amongst horses every day and I am constantly humbled and amazed by their sensitivity and athleticism, the acuity of their senses and the adaptive aspects of their mental abilities. It is my hope that by the end of this book you too will be similarly captivated.

And Ricky?

It took us nearly two years to quell the bulk of his anxiety – anxiety that I must be quick to point out was not caused by cruelty but, rather, by a training system that is anchored to tradition rather than evidence. Underneath all the stress, Ricky was a delightful, sensitive horse who was a pleasure to be around. For many years until his death at 25 years of age he was a reliable and much-loved pony club mount. I will always be grateful to him.

PART 1:

LETTING GO OF ANTHROPOMORPHISM

A few years ago, while travelling in Indonesia, a man approached me and asked if I would like to take my three children swimming with manta rays. I agreed — it was a beautiful day and as we talked I watched the children swim in the warm turquoise water, the sun bright and high above us. The next day, though, was cloudy and the surface of the ocean was slick and dark. The four of us and Wayan, the boatman, set off in a little wooden boat with the paint peeling off, the ancient outboard stuttering and a plastic water bottle half full of fuel wedged under the seat. We followed the coast around, watching the waves spend themselves on the beach, their tips feathered by the wind.

Eventually Wayan cut the throttle at the base of a cliff and the little boat rocked on the swell, just the sound of waves against the rock and the water under the hull. He pointed at the water 50 metres from the boat and we saw the triangular tip of a ray's wing, like a small dorsal fin, breaking the glassy surface. My youngest son pulled at my sleeve and pointed to the water — below the boat were swimming shadows, dark and shifting in the deep green water.

Wayan nodded at us and we pulled on our masks and eased ourselves into the ocean, holding onto the bobbing edge of the boat, smiling nervously at each other through our snorkels. After a few long moments my eldest son put his head under the water and I watched him kick himself away from the boat. Taking a deep breath I did the same, with the two younger children by my side. Somehow, it seemed lighter beneath the surface of the water; slivers of sun made their way through the clouds down to the sandy seabed and the sea was clear like glass around us. And the mantas. There were a dozen or more, each one as wide as an adult is tall, trailing small fish and bridal trains of bubbles. Like giant aquatic birds they flew, their great wings unfurled and the silver of their bellies shining. Turning on their sides as they passed us, close enough to touch.

We swam until we were chilled through and shivering, eventually pulling ourselves back into the boat, our faces aching from smiling at this glimpse of an amazing underwater world.

~

Our human desire to create narrative is an adaptive trait because, throughout time, it has served as a way to pass along vital information, which helped to keep our ancestors safe and fed and which, in turn, helped them to successfully raise families. Good examples of this are the songlines of the Indigenous Australians. These incredibly detailed and complex navigational stories have been used to pass down information through hundreds of generations. Using nothing more than these ancient stories and the stars, Aboriginal people could safely navigate hundreds of kilometres to find water and follow seasonal sources of food. And these stories are remarkably resilient. First Nations people in the southwest of Western Australia have oral stories that record the end of the last Ice Age — that's over 20,000 years ago.

The songlines survive countless generations because they are a valuable way of passing down vital information. In the same way, a lot of the myths and stories that exist in our culture today do so because at some time they served a purpose other than just entertainment. Fairytales, which may seem like simple narratives to entertain children, are actually cautionary tales designed to deliver important life lessons. For example, *Little Red Riding Hood* cautions children not to talk to strangers (especially those with hairy faces and long, sharp teeth) and *The Three Little Pigs* is a reminder that laziness can have dire repercussions.

When a story or its underlying theme becomes widespread it can become what psychologists call an heuristic — you can also call it a rule of thumb or an educated guess. It's a simple, efficient rule that we can use to make quick judgments when we're not in possession of all the facts. Heuristics are a form of mental shorthand that allow us to think on our feet and, most of the time, they're very handy. However, they do, on occasion, prompt us to make incorrect assumptions. This is known as cognitive bias and occurs when we make false conclusions based on our previous understanding of the world.

Anthropomorphism — the tendency to attribute human characteristics to animals — is an example of an heuristic because it allows us to make quick decisions about animal behaviour and motivation when we are not in possession of all the necessary facts. Yet, because of our long history with the horse, this is prone to cognitive bias or, in other words, false conclusions based on our own and others' past experiences. This explains how some ideas can infiltrate our popular ideology and become heuristics even though the notions that underpin them are both fictional and irrelevant.

Let's consider the horse whisperer, an idea that revolves around the belief that some people have a special ability to communicate with horses. This idea has its origins in medieval times when many thousands of people were tried as witches. Witches were sometimes drowned, hanged or burned at the stake, so it wasn't just that witchcraft was unfashionable, it was fatal. Horse trainers, particularly those who were skilled, would train in secret, just in case they were accused of witchcraft.

Although the killing stopped, the secrecy remained. The eighteenth century saw the arrival of secret societies such as the Horseman's Word — a society to which only men could be admitted and only then after special initiation ceremonies that included, amongst other things, reading passages of the Bible backwards. The Horseman's Word was like a trade union that protected trade secrets and taught its members various methods to control both horses and women. After a certain time the members of the Horseman's Word were told a secret word that, when whispered into a horse's ear, would make even the most unmanageable horse docile. It is from this that the term horse whisperer is derived. Despite its origins, the concept of the horse whisperer refuses to fade because it taps into an ancient and enduring heuristic that is based on anthropomorphism.

As an interesting aside, in 1865 six Confederate soldiers, who had emigrated to Tennessee from Scotland and who were familiar with the secret horse whispering societies, decided to set up their own group based on the same ideals. They decided to call it Kuklos, from the Greek word for circle. This secret group would change its focus over time and would eventually become the Ku Klux Klan — an unfortunate association that most of those who claim to be horse whisperers today would be unlikely to claim.

Anthropomorphism exists because it allows us to make assumptions about an animal whose mental state we have, until recently, known very little about. It makes sense that we should turn to our own experience of the world to interpret the actions and motivations of another species. Empathy is one of our most admirable human traits. However, it is also the one most likely to create cognitive bias when trying to unravel the mysteries of animal behaviour because we can only look at the world of an animal through the lens of our specifically human experience. This cognitive bias has led to some fairly significant misunderstandings between our species.

When we look at the horse through the objective lens of science rather than the subjective expectations of anthropomorphism, we see a reality so much more complex and amazing that it is like discovering an entirely new world. Letting go of anthropomorphism can be difficult. It is far easier to cling to the familiarity of old ideas and deeply held beliefs. But we miss out on so much of the wonder of the animal kingdom when we assume that animals are just like us — because beneath our anthropomorphism is a failure to acknowledge the unique qualities and abilities that have been bequeathed by evolution to each and every species.

After several thousand years of domestication it's inevitable that a certain degree of anthropomorphism has crept in to the relationship we have with our domesticated animals. And perhaps, like familiarity, anthropomorphism breeds contempt. Or, if not contempt, then at least a certain degree of complacency. After all, when we only ever view animals through the lens of anthropocentrism they seem like furry, lesser versions of ourselves. They can't talk, they can't drive cars, they can't update their Facebook status. But what an anthropocentric perspective fails to acknowledge is that if the boot was on the other foot (or hoof or paw or wing) it would be us who were lesser versions of them. How slowly we run. How blind and deaf we are. How badly we fly.

I sometimes think that if we had an entirely new language with which to talk about our animals we would be less inclined to compare them with ourselves. As an example, I'm always wary of the word 'intelligence' when it is related to horses because it is so loaded with all our human expectations and interpretations. I wonder if the meanings of such words are the sum total of our interactions with them — like a giant filing cabinet filled with snapshots of every usage, complete with prejudice and bias. When someone says to me, 'I don't think my horse is very intelligent,' I believe their statement is loaded, not just with the completely anthropocentric meaning of the word but also with the freight of their own personal history — their failed maths tests, lost keys and inability to decipher their new smartphone.

Memory is a similarly loaded concept when applied to horses because their memories are arranged and constructed so differently from our own. Here's an example ... There's a ditch at the end of my arena and occasionally I put jumps over it. It's a small change but the horses recognize it every time. The riders don't — they are usually a little bit frustrated that their horse, which last week didn't seem to mind the ditch at all, is this week rolling his eyes and snorting. It is almost as if we need separate words for the ways horses and humans store information from the past, because memory functions so differently in both species. I'm guessing that people can tell you where they were when they saw the first plane crash of 9/11 because of some primitive wiring in our brains that links shocking events with their location. But for the horse it seems that every single memory is intrinsically linked to the exact place where the memory was created.

In a way, I think the horse's memory is a lot more like a GPS than it is like ours. They are just so much better at knowing where they are in the landscape than we are. They notice and remember more detail. There are countless stories of horses finding their way home through snowstorms or at night, an ability that evolved because wild horses have a home range and, if the herd was scattered by a predator, the individuals would have to be able to find their way back there. When horses are being trained it's useful to tap into this ability. If I am training on the arena I will often set up marker cones or poles around a specific area, because once the horse has practised what it is they are learning in the designated space it becomes easier and easier to achieve in that space. If I then move the cones and poles (in the same exact pattern) to another part of the arena, the horse finds it easier to understand there what is required. The place itself becomes part of the cue for the behaviour. After several repetitions in different places you can remove the poles and the behaviour remains.

Even if we don't have a different vocabulary for speaking about horses it's still important to understand the ways in which the language we use crafts our reality. Just as it would be difficult to build a stealth bomber with parts recycled from a hang glider, it's difficult to describe our new evidence-based understanding of the horse using language that is hundreds, if not thousands, of years old. But if we're conscious of and vigilant about the meanings that words inadvertently bring to any conversation about the horse, then at least we are part of the way towards, if not eliminating, at least illuminating our inherent anthropomorphism.

As a very wise friend of mine once pointed out, none of us arrives at the side of the horse empty handed. The relationship between humans and horses is a little bit like a 6000-year-long marriage. Because the relationship is no longer driven by need, it's as though the kids have all grown up and left home and now it's just the two of us, sitting around the overly large dining room table trying to figure out exactly why it was that we fell in love in the first place. It's the perfect time to shed linguistic baggage, because it seems to me that the more we understand the creatures with whom we share our lives, the more we come to understand ourselves.

If we can let go of the assumptions that govern most of our interactions with the horse and embrace the science behind their physiology and behaviour, it's like diving under the water with manta rays. Putting your head under the water can be challenging at first, but once you have done it you will never look at the horse in the same way again.

THE DAWN HORSE

EOCENE EPOCH, 50 MILLION YEARS AGO

Beneath the canopy of tall trees the light is honey coloured, warm and heavy with unshed rain. It is almost silent in the forest, just the gentle sound of insects, the rustle of tiny creatures through leaf litter and the tinkling songs of small birds. The Dawn Horse's toed feet are light on the forest floor and the branches overhead make dark laced patterns on her spotted coat. She is the colour of shadows, of tree bark and low light through branches.

She is browsing on a patch of young ferns, nipping off the tender, unfurled shoots with her strong teeth, her jaws moving quickly from side to side. It is the start of the wet season and she is hungry; this the first patch of new ferns she has tasted for months and she is eager for the sweetness. Beside her are the six members of her family group, jostling and bumping each other as they forage together for the best shoots.

Although she is hungry the Dawn Horse stops from time to time to sniff the air, her fine nostrils flared for scent and her ears twitching for the sounds of predators. Savage dog-like Creodonts hunt in the twilight hours and their padded feet are almost silent in the leaf litter. In the waning light at the end of day their striped coats make them difficult to see and sometimes the only warning of their approach is the dead-flesh smell of their hot breath.

The Dawn Horse breathes the damp air for scent while watching the forest for signs of movement. She listens to the birds above her, fearing most of all the silence that might signal the approach of a predator, and only returns to eating when she is sure nothing in the forest has changed.

The small band of horses strips bare the patch of ferns. They are nuzzling the remaining fronds with their fine muzzles and searching for any missed shoots, when the Dawn Horse notices that the birds have fallen silent. She is instantly alert, raising her short neck, her eyes wide with fear. Sensing the tremor of a heavy footstep approaching she fills her lungs, tasting the air for the scent of a predator. In the sudden quiet a stick cracks under the foot of a bigger creature, and the Dawn Horse wheels around and bolts away. Behind her she hears the sound of heavy paws tearing through undergrowth, branches breaking and the high-pitched squeal of a panicked horse. But she is running, the muscles in her hindquarters bunching, weaving through the trees with her little neck outstretched and her slender legs extended.

~

It is almost dark by the time she slows her gallop, chest heaving and dark coat streaked with sweat. She hides in the deep shadows beneath an ancient beech tree until her breath settles and, smelling another member of her band close by, draws him to her with a low nicker. They stand with their shoulders and hips brushing together for comfort, touching each other every few breaths with their muzzles, silent as the night falls.

It is dawn before they dare to leave their hiding place, picking their way back through the forest towards the thickly wooded place where their herd has always sheltered. The land they move through is unfamiliar and they are wary, taking each careful step on pointed toes, their short, bony tails twitching with anxiety. By the time they are back in the densely treed hollow where the herd sleeps the sun is almost overhead. She sees that in the deep shadows of ancient trees there are three others from her herd, and she gives a low breathy neigh of greeting.

Later, while the others doze, she sniffs the air and watches the forest for change, sleeping only in short snatches. She is hungry and tired but her instinct will not let her rest. In the past few days she has felt a heaviness and a familiar stirring in her belly and she knows that soon there will be another small horse beside her. Another fragile life to take care of and watch over. But she will survive because she is careful. She is vigilant.

She is Eohippus, the Dawn Horse.

1.

THE ANCIENT HORSE

The story of *Equus caballus* — the modern horse — did not begin with domestication. It began 55 million years ago in the dense, humid forests of the Eocene Epoch, a time when our ancestors were still furry and swinging through the trees. While the horse's ancient, dog-sized ancestors may not seem particularly relevant today, to truly understand the modern horse, it is necessary to begin by viewing it through the lens of antiquity, because not only does the horse retain many of the characteristics bequeathed to it by its ancient ancestors, those traits still shape the interactions between our species.

The first horses were called Eohippus, which means Dawn Horse, and they were about the size of a labrador with four toes on each front foot and three on each back foot. Eohippus lived in marshy jungles and their toes, coupled with their petite stature, allowed them to skate lightly over the top of the leaf litter on the forest floor and avoid getting bogged in the mud. These small, early horses were extremely successful and, over time, they evolved into all sorts of other small horses which multiplied and spread to every continent of the world except Australia and Antarctica.

Although we usually think of the horse as a grazing animal, early horses ate leaves and fruit because, in the first few million years of their evolution, grass did not exist. Grass appeared in the Miocene Epoch, which started about 23 million years ago, and it was during this era that grasslands and savannahs gradually replaced the steamy forests and mega trees of previous times. Horses had to adapt to the challenges of their changing environment and, interestingly, some of those adaptations remain with them today.

In order to eat grass the horse developed the long teeth that modern horses still have. These are called hypsodont teeth and they continually erupt from the horse's gums, which makes them well suited to breaking down the tough fibres of grass and shrubs and coping with the extensive chewing and sandy grit that is the inevitable by-product of grazing and browsing.

The horse's digestive system also evolved to cope with the new grass diet. The cecum, which is essentially just a large, muscular fermentation vat in the horse's gut where cellulose is digested, appeared in the variety of early horse known as

Merychippus about 15 million years ago. The cecum equipped Merychippus to meet the challenge of this new and plentiful feed source by not only extracting as many nutrients from the grass as possible, but also enabling the horse to cover long distances without the need to rest after feeding, unlike ruminants such as cows, sheep and goats, which must lie down to chew their cud for several hours each day.

But perhaps one of the most significant challenges faced by early horses was the need for speed. It's hard to hide on a grassy plain and early horses had to develop ways to avoid being eaten. Over time horses gradually lost their toes and began to walk (and run) on what had once been their middle toe. Merychippus and Mesohippus had three toes, but little Pliohippus (appearing about 10 million years ago) had just one. Pliohippus was the most direct ancestor of *Equus caballus* and they were the first of the ancient horses to become monodactyl – single toed.

All modern equines (including horses, donkeys and zebras) belong to the genus Equus and this group of horses first appeared about 4.5 million years ago. Equus is adapted for speed, and while a cheetah will beat a horse over a short distance, in a longer race the horse is one of the fastest animals on the planet. One of the ways horses achieve this speed is by walking on the tip of their single toe, which gives them extra length in the lower part of their limbs – a conformation often associated with speed. Their slender but extremely strong leg bones can withstand the pressures of galloping, and elastic digital ligaments in their lower limbs flex with movement and act as a kind of energy-gathering spring. Equus also has very limited lateral (side to side) limb movements, another adaptation that contributes to their great speed.

Another way the horse is adapted for speed over longer distances is through what is called locomotor-respiratory coupling. This means that at faster gaits (canter and gallop) the horse breathes once for every stride. The internal organs of the horse are suspended by elastic structures within the body and act a little like a piston inside a cylinder, drawing air into the lungs and pushing it out again. During the moment in the stride when all the horse's legs are off the ground the organs slide backwards, drawing air into the lungs. As the stride progresses and the head and neck move downwards, the organs slide forwards and the air is expelled. Horses are obligate nose breathers, which means they cannot breathe through their mouths, yet the peak airflow when galloping is still around 80 litres (21 gal) per second. This makes them highly efficient at speed over a long distance.

Although early members of the Equus genus stood little over 12 hands high (approximately 122 centimetres/48 in tall at the base of the neck) the modern horse still retains many of the physical and mental characteristics that evolved millions of years ago. As well as being monodactyl (one digit per limb), and possessing hypsodont teeth and a cecum, our modern horses still retain many of the features of their forest-dwelling forebears. In the modern horse the two extra toes of Merychippus have become the splint bones either side of the canon bone, while Merychippus's toenails have become the modern horse's chestnuts and ergots (the horny nubbles of skin on the surface of the legs). Our horse's peg-like wolf teeth are the leftovers of two extra premolars that were used to chew bark and leaves before the evolution of grass.

We can see the horse's unique evolution in some of the conformation traits that are present today. The long, flexible neck of modern horses is a little like a periscope and it evolved so that they could easily watch over their surroundings, while their large, side-mounted eyes made them difficult to sneak up on. This is also why the horse has amazingly acute hearing, smell and vision that spans almost 270 degrees. These all contribute to the horse's two best defence strategies: speed and vigilance.

Fight, flight and freeze response

The horse's evolution has bequeathed to it many instincts related to survival. Two of these instincts — the flight response and the herd instinct — are fundamental to its makeup. The flight response is sometimes called the flight or fight response, but it could more correctly be called the flight, fight or freeze response because all horses will revert to one of the three Fs when frightened. As Dr Andrew McLean has pointed out, early horses evolved in two largely separate forms — those that were adapted to be chased by members of the big cat family, and those adapted to be chased by members of the dog family. If you're going to get attacked by a lion you run away because lions can only sustain top speed for a few hundred metres. If you're going to get attacked by wolves you stand and fight because few things can outrun a pack of cooperatively hunting canines. The modern horse is a mix of both forms but one will usually dominate. So, many of the lighter breeds such as thoroughbreds and Arabs are more inclined towards flight, while some of the heavier breeds are more inclined towards fight. Some horses will momentarily freeze (stand absolutely still) when frightened but after several seconds will usually launch into flight mode.

The flight response is an ancient instinct that, nevertheless, is still a significant part of the horse's makeup. It's the way the horse deals with fear. The flight response is mediated by the sympathetic nervous system, which triggers the release of adrenaline and noradrenaline. This in turn triggers the HPA (hypothalamic-pituitary-adrenal gland) axis, which results in the production of corticotropin releasing hormone (CRH), which is a little bit like fuel for the flight response. This then starts a cascade of changes in the brain, and, if the stress continues for longer than a couple of minutes, triggers the release of cortisol. Cortisol causes many changes in the body that enable it to deal with challenging situations. These changes include increased blood pressure, a release of glucose from the liver and enhanced memory of the fearful stimulus.

The problem with the flight response in horses is that we don't always recognize it and it can be insidious. The flight response can show up in very subtle ways and yet, if allowed to continue unchecked, it can have really unpleasant long-term consequences for the horse. It's a little bit like a human with severe anxiety. Exhibiting the flight response is stressful for the horse. Chronic stress causes baseline levels of cortisol to rise and an over-activation of the HPA axis. Over time this can contribute to a suppressed immune system and a predisposition towards metabolic conditions, not to mention a significant reduction in welfare.

The flight response can be as subtle as quickening steps, a high head carriage, tension or a tightly clamped tail. Or it can be as obvious as bucking, rearing, shying, spinning and rushing jumps. The ultimate expression of the flight response is full blown bolting which, luckily, is quite rare because a truly bolting horse is a danger to itself and everyone around it.

When trainers use anthropomorphic explanations of behaviour and don't train in ways that minimize the flight response, the horse's welfare suffers. A child's pony rushing around a jumping course with a high head carriage is in the grip of the same cascade of stress hormones as a zebra running from a lion. And just as you would expect with the zebra, they generally don't 'get over it'; in fact, one of the effects of cortisol on the brain means that whatever triggered the fear can be remembered after just one exposure. We call this 'single trial learning' and it's a great way for the horse to remember how to escape from things that would like to eat it — but in a training context, this can be problematic.

It can be tricky to recognize the flight response in training but a good indicator is the presence of quickening steps. The best of the classical masters of dressage training as far back as the seventeenth century instinctively knew this and they prioritized what has become known as self-carriage. This means that the horse maintains its speed and line without the need for constant reminders from the rider. Traditionally, the rider on the charging, reefing horse has been viewed as skilful or brave, but in reality they are allowing a situation that is problematic to the horse's welfare to continue unchecked.

Herd instinct

The other instinct that forms a fundamental part of the horse's 'horseness' is the herd instinct. For horses, nothing is truer than the statement that there's safety in numbers. The horse is driven by its instincts to form strong bonds with other horses because the herd is intrinsic to the horse's safety. Even though very few domestic horses have to contend with wolves or lions, the herd instinct remains. Horses need other horses in the same way that humans need other humans. Lengthy periods of solitary confinement are identified as inhumane by the Geneva Convention because social isolation is extremely stressful for social mammals.

Horses form lifelong bonds with members of their herd and their interactions are subtle and complex. They are extremely tactile and will often spend hours mutually grooming each other in the few places on their bodies they can't reach themselves. So important are the bonds between herd members that this mutual grooming lowers the horse's heart rate and blood pressure. It even works when we groom the same sites. Luckily for us these are conveniently located where a rider can reach them — either side of the wither, at the base of the neck.

It's far more rewarding for the horse if we scratch and stroke her neck than if we pat it. Patting, let's be honest, is way more about us than the animal anyway. Patting is a very human behaviour and I've yet to see animals of any species pat each other as a way of expressing connection, but licking, rubbing scratching and stroking are all pretty common. Even humans don't really like to be patted (if we did we'd pay the masseuse not to rub us but to pat us).

Why the long face?

The reason for the horse's long face can also be found in evolution. If it were possible to measure the average height of grass 20 million years ago, I'd guess that it would correlate pretty well with the average distance from incisor to eye of Pliohippus and its descendants. The horse's eyes are positioned at the top of an elongated head because this allows him to look over the top of grass while grazing, which means he can eat and still remain vigilant to the approach of predators. And even though most of those predators became extinct a long, long time ago, DNA has an indelible memory when it comes to survival tactics. The horse's long face is a daily reminder for those of us who work with them that we are asking a prehistoric brain to solve 21st-century problems.

That horses have retained their long faces and many other features of their timid but speedy ancestors sends a clear message to us as their custodians: you can take the horse out of the wilderness but you can never completely take the wildness out of the horse. Beneath the fluffy coat of even the most beloved and docile child's pony lie the senses and instincts that kept its ancestors safe from predators all those millions of years ago.

ANCIENT MAN

WEST KAZAKHSTAN, 5500 YEARS AGO

Spring came early to the valley and the snow has started melting. Ancient man leans against the earth wall of his hut and looks out at the bare patches of ground where he knows that soon the grass will grow. He also knows that soon the wild horses will find their way back to the valley to graze and he is pleased, because even though the winter had been mild he is tired of frozen, salted meat and is looking forward to fresh.

Like his father before him, he kept a small number of horses in a wooden corral during the winter. He had caught them in the autumn as the leaves were falling, mostly youngsters and mares with foals at foot. During the long, dark days of winter they milked the mares, tying up their deadly hooves with thongs of leather and eventually, when their supply of salted meat ran out, they would kill and eat them. But the past winter had been mild and short and now the snow is melting there are still four brown horses standing quietly in the yard. All through the winter he had fed them gathered grains and dried grass until they were used to him, sometimes even calling out as he walked past their enclosure.

Ancient man watches the horses in the yard. He is troubled by a dream that has been waking him at night since the thaw began. In his dream he sees himself sitting astride one of the mares, the ground flashing beneath her hooves and her thick, wiry mane in his hands. He knows it is the gods who send dreams to people, sometimes to warn them and sometimes to offer instruction. His dream, he believes, is an instruction.

For days he spends his time watching the horses in the yard, angering his wife who would have liked him to cut wood for the fire or hack apart the ice-bound meat they have stored beneath the ground. She also yells at him for spending too much time making leather ropes, sawing and twisting them back and forth along the sharpened jaw bone of a moose until they are straight and strong in his hands.

He has already chosen which of the horses to ride. A big, round-bodied mare — the easiest of the four to milk and so tame that some days she even takes grain from his hand. Despite himself, he likes the feel of her warm muzzle on his skin and the smell of her breath when she is close. In his dream he sees her with leather straps around her head and he holds the loops with his hands while he watches her, imagining the knots he would tie.

He takes a deep breath, looks around to make sure his wife isn't watching and climbs into the yard. The horses shuffle around to face him, curious but not frightened. From inside his skins he takes a handful of grain and holds it out to the big mare with a loop of rope hidden behind his back. She is cautious but hungry, leaning over her front legs and stretching her neck as far as possible. Ancient man is not as fast as the horse but he is skilled with a rope and his hands are strong from years of work. Before the mare can run away he throws a loop of rope around her neck and takes the ends in both of his hands. She plunges and bucks but she was milked many times over the winter and eventually she stands quietly, looking at him.

He works his way down the rope towards her, hand over hand, stretching his arm out when he is close enough and feeling her thick, dusty coat. He finds himself quietly singing one of the songs his wife sings to soothe their babies to sleep, and he looks around quickly to make sure no one is watching him. Standing at the side of the big mare, looking at the power of her muscles and the width of her shoulders, he can feel his heart beating, half fear, half excitement. With a nod to the gods and a quick, deep breath he swings himself onto her back. For a moment she is still and he sees the sky big above him and the light on the fields of snow. He can see further from on her back, over the top of his low house and into the forest beyond, and he feels like singing again.

Suddenly, with a deep roaring breath, the mare lurches forwards. Her head goes down between her knees and she bucks. Ancient man is strong and he clings to her mane with all of his strength, but after just two bucks he feels himself airborne, landing with a heavy thud on the ground of the muddy yard. He brushes the clinging mud from his skins with a quick smile — he isn't really sure how he'll explain it to his wife but he doesn't have the time to stop and think of excuses. With deep creases between his eyes, he looks at the mare in the yard and the straps he has tied around her head. He knows if he can stop her from putting her head down he might have a chance of staying on her back. He thinks about the horse jaw bones that his people used to scrape leather with. There is a gap between the biting teeth at the front and the chewing ones behind, and he suddenly realizes that a strap through her mouth might give him the control he needs.

He catches the mare in the yard and quietly adjusts the leather harness he had made. She fights him when he tries to get the leather in her mouth and he is flung around like a falling leaf in the wind but is able to get it done at last. He is glad the gods didn't want him to ride one of the moose that roam the valley over summer — the mare's back is level with his chest but a moose is taller than his shoulders and has sharp, hard antlers that could easily kill a wolf or a man driven to foolish extremes by mid-winter dreams.

Again he takes a deep breath and leaps onto the mare's back. Again she roars and bucks but this time he is able to keep her head up and the bucks are not as high. He sits about five minutes before flying through the air and landing in the mud. Ancient man's body aches all over from where he hit the ground but he can see that the mare is tiring after a winter spent in the small yard. He catches her again quickly and leaps up onto her again. She bucks and roars but he manages to keep her head up. She tries galloping around the yard, pushing her way past the other horses and rubbing his leg on the rails, but he clings tightly to her mane until eventually she slows.

After a while she stops running and walks quietly amongst the other horses. Ancient man allows himself a small smile, his heart beating and his bruises not yet sore enough to bother him. He slides from her back and pulls the harness from her head. She stands next to him for a moment and he reaches into his skins to find one last small handful of grain to feed to her. As she chews, he reaches out and touches her sweaty neck, feeling the warmth of her and something else too — a kind of gratitude that together they have fulfilled the wishes of the gods. He strokes her fur like he would stroke the hair of his children and she stands for his touch, almost, he thinks, as though she enjoys it.

He leans on the fence, feeling the sky bigger and bluer than he has ever seen it and the sun on the snow and the singing of the first birds in the forest. He stretches his arms out wide and feels the cool air enter him; he knows he will be as stiff as his grandfather tomorrow, but today he is happy. He climbs out through the rails and sees his wife standing, watching him. She looks so surprised that she might as well be watching him fly like a bird. He walks past, looking at her hanging jaw and the wide open circles of her eyes. And just before he bends down to enter the small, low doorway of his hut, he turns his face to her and closes one eye in a slow, deliberate wink.

2.

THE DOMESTICATED HORSE

While it would be difficult to find an event more significant in the history of humanity than the domestication of the horse, it is also the most significant moment in the history of the horse, because it is in that moment that the future of the species was assured. By the end of the last Ice Age, roughly 18,000 years ago, early horses were extinct in North America and very close to extinction in Europe and Asia as well. Had domestication not occurred, it is likely that the horse would only exist today in museums alongside other evolutionary cul de sacs like pterodactyls and *Tyrannosaurus rex*.

Before the Ice Age, early horses like Eohippus were very successful and, eventually, they roamed over most of what is now North America, Europe and Asia. But the last Ice Age (from

2.4 million to roughly 18,000 years ago) offered challenges the horse was not equipped to deal with. To comfortably survive inhospitable cold, it is useful to be enormous (like a mammoth) or to cover yourself in thick fur (like a giant ground sloth). At a little under 100 kilograms (220 lb) the small, fleet Nannippus was neither large nor generously furred. And the same can be said of the ten or so other prehistoric Equus species that lived at the start of the Ice Age. After the Ice Age, fossilized horse remains became quite scarce and it was not until after domestication that this trend reversed.

Horses were certainly not the first animals to be domesticated; in fact, they were relative latecomers. Dogs began living alongside humans about 12,000 years ago, sheep and goats 10,000 years ago, cats 9000 years ago, cattle 8000 years ago, camelids (camels, alpacas and llamas) 7500 years ago, and the horse and elephant about 6000 years ago. It is difficult to know what would have happened to these species if domestication had not occurred, but an insight can be gained from the history of the two subspecies of Equus that were not domesticated.

Przewalski's horses

It's important to note that the brumbies and mustangs we think of as wild are the offspring of domestic horses that escaped and became feral. Only two truly wild subspecies of *Equus caballos* have survived beyond the nineteenth century. The Tarpan (*Equus ferus ferus*) was hunted mercilessly and declared extinct in 1919, and Przewalski's horse (*Equus ferus przewalskii*) survives in small numbers and only because of a remarkable effort made by zoos around the world to save them. In contrast, the domesticated horse population is massive, with numbers around the world estimated to be in excess of 60 million.

It used to be believed that Przewalski's (pronounced *sher vol skeze*) horses were the distant ancestors of the domestic horse, a more ancient form of the same species. However, we now know that they are genetically quite different. While they share a common ancestor, their evolutionary paths diverged about 50,000 years ago. These small horses have creamy-coloured coats with a lighter belly and white muzzle. They have distinctive black, upright manes, short legs and a large head with an egg-shaped profile.

Przewalski's horses once roamed the Mongolian steppes of the Gobi Desert and were hunted almost to extinction in their homeland. Very small populations survived in zoos and safari parks but their numbers had dwindled by the beginning of the twentieth century. At the end of World War II the few that were left in European zoos were eaten by hungry soldiers. By 1946 there were just 31 of these horses left and by the early

1950s that number had shrunk to just twelve – and only nine of those were of breeding age (one stallion and eight mares). The Zoological Society of London, in conjunction with Mongolian researchers, embarked on a program to rescue the world's only surviving truly wild horse.

Luckily for the Przewalski's horses, although they have 66 chromosomes and the domestic horse has 64, their offspring are almost always fertile. Donkeys have 62 chromosomes and the offspring of donkeys and horses (mules and hinnies) are almost always infertile. In the early days of the rescue effort, researchers were able to use occasional outcrosses of wild horses with Mongolian domesticated mares of very similar type, and this has prevented a complete lack of genetic diversity.

By the 1990s the numbers of Przewalski's horses had climbed to over 1500 individuals and they have been successfully reintroduced to several national parks in what was once their native habitat. In 2018 it was estimated that the world's population was just in excess of 2000 horses, and over 300 of them have been reintroduced to the wild. Strangely enough, one of the places where they are really thriving is the Chernobyl exclusion zone. After the failure of the Chernobyl nuclear reactor in 1986 a 30-kilometre (18½ mi) exclusion zone around the site was evacuated and this remains almost totally uninhabited by humans. However, it appears that the animal population is thriving and showing few ill effects from the high levels of radiation. Elk, roe deer, wild boar, brown bears, wolves and Przewalski's horses are flourishing in what was once a busy town. Although still classified as critically endangered, the future for Przewalski's horses is looking a lot more certain than it did three or four decades ago.

How domestication occurred

Archaeologists, surprisingly, are quite argumentative. Exactly where and how the horse was domesticated is still hotly debated. The one thing archaeologists do agree on, however, is that it occurred about 6000 years ago.

It seems likely that our ancestors first used horses for both meat and to ride. This is because, without fencing, it is almost impossible to herd and control large numbers of horses unless you're mounted. The first evidence we have of bit use comes from Dereivka, an ancient village in what is modern-day Ukraine. In this village archaeologists found the 6000-year-old skull of a horse (probably belonging to a seven- or eight-year-old stallion), accompanied by two pieces of antler with holes bored in them. Although initially they were puzzled by these strange artefacts, the archaeologists eventually realized they were the cheek pieces of an ancient bridle and would have held a thong of leather or plaited rope in place. Subsequent experiments have shown that these ancient bridles actually work quite efficiently in the mouths of modern horses.

But more importantly, the Dereivka stallion showed a wear pattern on his teeth that only exists amongst horses that are ridden or driven with a bit in their mouths. When a bit is correctly adjusted in a horse's mouth, it is supposed to sit in the interdental space (the place in the horse's mouth without teeth, between the front incisors and back molars). X-ray pictures of bitted horses nonetheless show that they often avoid bit pressure by holding the bit between their molars. This way they can hold the bit with their very strong jaws and limit the amount of pressure that can be applied to their sensitive lips and tongue. In almost all riding horses, microscopic examination of the teeth reveals a bevelled front edge of the premolars. This wear pattern is not consistent with normal side-to-side grinding caused by chewing, and is not seen in wild horse populations. The Dereivka stallion showed wear patterns on his teeth exactly the same as the wear patterns on the teeth of modern riding horses.

Recent experiments have shown that when previously unhandled horses are mouthed and ridden in bits modelled on those found in Dereivka, with either leather or rope mouthpieces, the wear patterns are the same as those seen on the 6000-year-old skull. This is extraordinary because, in the context of human history, it means that the bit was invented at least 500 years before the wheel.

However, this evidence is not enough for some archaeologists, who claim that the horse was first domesticated in a place called Botai in Kazakhstan. Large heavy stones that could have only come from a quarry 50 miles away have been found at the Botai site, which suggests that the residents of Botai had ways of transporting heavy things. Archaeologists have also found full horse skeletons in burial sites, suggesting they may have been sacrificed and buried alongside their humans. This definitely points to domestication, because even the smaller horses of 6000 years ago would have weighed at least 400 kilograms (63 st). This makes it unlikely that they were hunted on the plains and then dragged to the burial site intact. Most interestingly of all, though, archaeologists found that the Botai people left great numbers of leatherworking tools. It's easy to imagine that when people with little or no training experience attempted to tame wild horses there would be lots of broken ropes and therefore many leather working tools required to repair it.

It seems likely, given the evidence, that the domestication of the horse occurred at least twice: once in what is now Ukraine and once in what is now Kazakhstan. Regardless of where it happened or which occurred first, the domestication of the horse not only allowed ancient humans to travel long distances and lift heavy things, it also allowed them to control and move large herds of livestock. The concentrated and easy-to-manage food source this afforded our ancestors changed forever the structure of human society, because it meant they could stay in one place and still have enough to eat. When Neil Armstrong first walked on the moon he said, 'That's one small step for man, one giant leap for mankind'. The first person to ever ride a horse should have said something similarly inspiring because quite simply, after that moment, the world would never be the same place again.

Why horses and not moose or giraffes?

There are over 4000 species of mammal that have lived on earth in the last 10,000 years and the horse is one of a handful of large mammals that have been successfully domesticated. Over the centuries we have tried to domesticate lots of different animals including antelope, ibex, gazelles, raccoons, bears, wallabies, kangaroos and even moose, but there have been only a few success stories. In the case of horses, the answer to why lies in the characteristics of the horse that make domestication possible and even simple. The horse already possessed these characteristics prior to domestication, so in a sense it was preadapted through some quirks of evolution.

The horse can survive on a variety of widely available foods, which makes it far easier to manage than an animal that is dependent on only one food source, such as the koala. Travel to new continents would be difficult using koalas as pack animals. Their diet is 99 per cent eucalyptus leaves, and of the 900 different eucalypts in Australia there are only ten that the koala deems edible. Travelling with a large number of koalas and trying to keep them all well fed would be a logistical nightmare.

Unlike swans and beavers, the horse does not mate for life, and a stallion is more than happy to mate with multiple mares in a single breeding season. This means is it relatively simple to change the characteristics of a population by breeding for certain traits. Stallions with desirable characteristics can be bred to a large number of mares in a season and their offspring have a relatively good chance of inheriting at least some of those desirable traits. Also, horses don't build giant, tree-damming lodges, burrows, warrens or even nests, which makes pregnant equines and young stock relatively mobile. The horse is not territorial, unlike wolves or cougars, which means it is happy to move beyond its ancestral range.

The horse's herbivorous diet is also a distinct advantage — polar bears, which are often in the same weight range as horses (up to 650 kg/102 st), can eat up to 40 kilograms of meat in a single meal, making them expensive (and dangerous) livestock. The horse is mono-gastric, which means it has one stomach, whereas ruminants like sheep and cattle have four. This form of digestion (bequeathed to the modern horse by Merychippus) allows it to break down the otherwise indigestible cellulose in grass and allows the horse to eat and run, unlike ruminants which must lie down after eating in order to chew their cud.

The horse's lack of horns, tusks and antlers is also a big plus for domestication because it makes them easy to handle. And lastly, one of the most important physical characteristics that made domestication possible is the horse's external testes, which make him easier to castrate than armadillos, sloths and elephants, whose testes remain within the abdomen. Humans have been gelding horses since the Scythians discovered how to do it around the ninth century BCE. These nomadic tribes roamed the Eurasian steppe for about fifteen centuries and the practice of castrating horses continues to this day because, as the Scythians discovered, geldings are often less distracted than stallions.

EZIO

GREECE,
12TH CENTURY BCE

Although his joints are stiff with age, Ezio takes the path to the stables to watch his youngest grandsons, Leon and Zeno, riding their horses. He walks slowly down from the house through a grove of olive trees as bent and gnarled as an old man so many summers past his three score years and ten that it is no longer worth counting. Leaning heavily on his cypress staff, his bare feet are slow on the uneven path and barely raise the dust.

The meadow where the boys ride is large and ringed with ancient orange trees. Ezio can smell the perfume of their leaves in the late afternoon sun and he smiles and breathes the memories of their scent deep into his lungs. As a boy, he had ridden where his grandsons now ride and he remembers how, after a day spent inside scratching numbers and words onto wax, he would gallop his horse until his shadow was long on the ground and the sweet smell of citrus faded with the day's last light.

He calls for a chair and one of the servants comes running. Another brings a filled cup and, though he is fairly certain his daughter-in-law has had the servants water his wine, he sips it and then sighs with satisfaction.

Though their voices are yet to break, the two boys are training for war, a light javelin in one hand and a leather shield in the other. Ezio watches with pride as they gallop and wheel their small horses around, sitting lightly and easily. They hurl their javelins at a wooden target and though their slight arms don't yet have much power he is pleased to see that their accuracy is improving.

Eventually the boys grow tired and they canter their horses to Ezio's chair.

'Did you see me hit the target, Grandfather?' says Zeno.

'And me too?' says Leon.

They slide off their horses and toss the reins to a waiting servant. Together they lean in and hug Ezio, and he smiles at their sweaty faces against his.

'You are both getting so big,' he says.

'Not too big for stories though, Grandfather,' says Leon.

'Yes,' says Zeno, nodding. 'Will you tell us the one about Troy?'

'Yes! The one about Troy,' says Leon.

'If you insist,' says Ezio happily. 'Sit down next to me in the long grass and I'll tell you what happened when Helen, the most beautiful woman in the world, was seduced and then abducted by Paris, the handsome Prince of Troy.'

He raises his empty cup at a passing servant and says, 'But first, more wine to soothe my parched throat.' And smiles at the servant as the wine is poured.

'Boys, my old bones will grow chilly once the sun disappears and you know this story already, so I'll make haste to begin,' he says and takes a long swallow of his wine.

'When Menelaus, the King of Sparta, discovered that his wife Helen had been stolen and taken to Troy he was furious and demanded her return. He sent an enormous army to Anatolia, confident that he would soon have her back, but it didn't quite work out the way he had planned.

'I joined the army when I was fifteen,' continues Ezio, 'like my father and his father before him, and by the time I arrived in Anatolia, just a boy and wet behind the ears, the war over Helen had been grinding on for seven long years. The Greek army threw everything it had at Troy but, still, it resisted them. The men on the beach were starting to believe that only divine intervention could open the city's gates and even Odysseus, the best and bravest soldier in all of Greece, seemed to have run out of ideas,' Ezio says, rubbing his chin.

'I have to say, when I stepped off the boat it looked like just another city to me. The walls were strong, raised from limestone and as thick at their base as they were high. And the gates were heavy wood and bound with steel, but to my young eyes it didn't look impossible. I was hopeful for a quick end to the war, little knowing it would be another three years before I would see my home and family again.'

Ezio looks down at his grandsons lying on the grass. Zeno is resting his head on Leon's shoulder and they both look up at the sky, eyes half closed against the last of the light.

'I hated that place. Even today, I still hate the sound of the name. I hated the sand flies that stung my skin like nettles. I hated digging latrines and cleaning armour. I hated the smell of barley porridge cooking and the feel of sand between my teeth. It was freezing cold on the edge of the Aegean Sea and our tents were so threadbare that I spent each night huddled, shivering, under my cloak on the sand. And you boys know how I hate the cold.

'Oh, how I missed my mother and my older sisters. At night I would dream of their laughter and of sleeping between linen sheets that smelled like sunshine. I couldn't wait to return home and drink the wine from our vines and taste the sweet oranges from this meadow. I couldn't wait to tell my family stories about my courage and daring — even though, if I'm honest, I spent most of my time working like a slave digging holes and dragging water barrels up the beach.'

Ezio looks at his grandsons and nods. 'In a camp full of hungry men rumours fly like autumn leaves. But one day, after three unhappy years, it seemed that finally something different was happening. Day after day teams of men were sent into the forest to fell trees, and for weeks afterwards all we could hear from dawn till dusk was the grind of huge logs being dragged into camp and the sawing of timber.

'In the centre of our camp, an area as big as this meadow had been flattened, and on the sand the engineer Epeius had drawn a horse as tall as two houses standing one on the other. His many calculations were marked in the sand and, as you boys know, the only thing I love more than your grandmother is numbers — and here were lists of them as long as my arm, calling to me as surely as a flower calls bees.

'Whenever I could shirk my duties, I would scurry to where Epeius was working and I would do his calculations in my head, letting the numbers flow over me like cool water at the end of a long hot day. One day I noticed that Epeius had added incorrectly and, because I was a stupid boy with more courage than sense, I told him. For a moment he said nothing and I was sure he was going to have me whipped. But then, finally, he smiled and the next day when I turned up at my post to begin yet another day of endless digging, the captain sent me away and told me I was to be the engineer's assistant.'

Ezio smiles at the memory and drains his cup.

'For weeks I was the engineer's right hand. If he thought it, I ran. If he said it, I ran faster. And slowly but surely out of the dusty sand of an Anatolian beach grew the most enormous wooden horse you could ever imagine. We worked the carpenters night and day and what a sight it was — they swarmed all over it, like ants on its giant body. Epeius had ordered a clever trapdoor to be hidden in the ribs of the beast and inside its giant belly there were benches for men to sit on. On the outside was carved "For their return home the Greeks dedicate this offering to Athena".

'The next day we broke camp. Burned our tents, collected our weapons, dismantled the kitchens and packed all our belongings into a fleet of ships that had gathered just off the coast. It seemed as though the war was about to end and, even though we had been beaten, I was excited.

'That night we lay down on the sand wrapped in our cloaks, happy that we would soon be on our way back home. I had just fallen asleep when Epeius woke me up with a hand on my shoulder. "It's time to see if the Trojans are fooled by our plan," he said and gestured for me to follow him up the beach to where, in the darkness, I could see men gathering next to the horse. Hurriedly and in silence we climbed a rope ladder up into the belly of the giant beast. There were at least thirty armed men already in there and I spotted some of the bravest soldiers in the army, including Odysseus.

'"If you and I have done our job properly," Epeius whispered to me, "the Trojans will accept our offering and drag it to the temple of Athena. But you must be very, very quiet because they cannot know that we are hidden in here."

'While I was hiding in the horse, shaking inside with fear and excitement, the rest of our army pretended to sail away, leaving the wooden horse alone on the beach. Although it felt like days to me, just a few hours later the Trojans came down to marvel at the enormous horse in front of their city. We sat so quietly in its belly that we could hear them arguing over what to do with it. When I heard one of the priests suggest that they burn it my heart started racing, but pretty soon they decided to drag it into the city and take it to the temple of Athena as an offering.'

Ezio leans forward, wine glass forgotten in his hand. 'The day was long and hot. Ropes creaked and we could hear dozens of slaves groaning as they struggled to drag the horse through the sand. I was worried the horse would be torn in two with the force. But the joints held and eventually we heard a creaking as the city gates opened and we felt the horse rolling more easily over the smoother surface of a road.

'We waited inside the horse for hours. It was like a sweat bath in there with so many bodies close together. We listened to the Trojan people admire our work and we breathed shallow and tried not to cough. Not long after the sun went down the city grew very quiet.

'At midnight Odysseus nodded at Epeius and together we opened the trapdoor and secured the rope ladder that was stashed under our seats. Silently the soldiers swung to the ground until just Epeius and I were left inside. We heard the creak of the city gates being opened and not long after that we heard the battle cry of the Greek army as the ships returned from where they had been hiding behind some islands just offshore.

'The battle that followed was fierce and bloody. Epeius decided we would stay inside the horse and protect it and around us we watched the men fight and the city in flames. By lunchtime the next day, Troy was plundered and Helen was on her way back to Sparta. Epeius and I climbed down from the horse and looked at the carnage around us.

'And then, striding out of the fire and smoke of the ruined city came Odysseus. Tall, strong and smeared with the blood of his enemies, he was a truly magnificent sight.

' "You did it, Epeius," he said. "And I shall forever be in your debt."

' "It was your idea," said my master graciously. "And a stroke of genius it was too."

'Odysseus shook his head modestly. "I simply asked myself what is so beautiful, so important and so necessary that even the Trojans cannot resist it?"

' "Of course," said Epeius, smiling. "What creature could unlock the gates of Troy when even the might of the Greek army couldn't? Only a horse!" '

Ezio takes another swallow of wine, smiles at his memories and leans down to smooth Leon's hair from his forehead.

'It was indeed a stroke of genius,' he says, almost to himself. 'There is nothing in this world as necessary and yet as beautiful as a horse.'

3.

THE IMPORTANT HORSE

In many ways the story of the Trojan horse, as well as illustrating the importance of the horse (in a practical, spiritual and cultural sense), is also a good metaphor for the relationship between our species. Just as the Trojan horse carried Odysseus and his men into the city of Troy, so too does the real horse carry the weight of our combined histories, our millennia of mutual need and our anthropocentric world view into the 21st century.

Acknowledging that this long and interwoven history might have muddied the waters between our species is almost certainly the first step towards solving the complex puzzle of how best to manage the horse both now and in the future. Even if you have never swung a leg over the back of the horse, thanks to fairytales and the Disney channel it is likely you arrive at his side bearing expectations and beliefs that the horse cannot possibly live up to.

This has meant that many management and training practices that exist today lead to both suboptimal welfare for the horse and increased levels of danger for riders and handlers. A horse can weigh in the vicinity of 600 kilograms (94 st), can gallop at 65 kilometres (40 mi) per hour and kick with a force of over 1.5 times its body weight. A recent survey on the number of fatalities per 100,000 participants in sports events per year in the United States put riding a horse at the top of the list with a substantial 128. In contrast, boxing has just 1.3 deaths per 100,000 per year. It has been shown that riders can be expected to suffer one injury for every 1000 hours of riding time, which makes equestrian sports more dangerous than motorcycle riding and car racing. In Australia, horse riders have been recognized in the Commonwealth Department of Human Service and Health's injury prevention strategy as one of four groups to be targeted in order to reduce severe injury and fatality.

The situation for the horse is not ideal, either. The wastage rates of both racing and performance horses are too high. In 1977, Professor Frank Odberg and Dr Marie Bouisseau highlighted the high rate of wastage in performance horses. Their study of French slaughterhouses revealed that 66.4 per cent of horses were in the abattoir for behavioural reasons, and most were between the ages of two and seven years old. In a later study at a Munich abattoir, they found that, of 2970 horses, 50 per cent were there for non-medical reasons and most were under five years of age. At an equitation science conference in 2006, I asked Professor Odberg if he thought the situation would have improved in the past 40 or so years and he replied that he believed it would be even more disturbing.

It's not just wastage that is a problem, either. When considering welfare it is important to examine the number of domestic horses that exhibit stereotypies (functionless, repetitive behaviours like the rocking from side to side, known as weaving), have gastric ulceration or manifest conflict behaviours such as fence walking, and aggressive behaviours such as kicking and biting — all of which suggest a suboptimal environment. One of the most extreme conflict behaviours, self-mutilation, is not unheard of amongst performance horses; indeed, on the internet it's possible to buy kevlar vests for horses to prevent them from damaging themselves. I have seen horses bite themselves on the chest during training and it is perhaps one of the most disturbing things I have seen in my 30-year career as a trainer. The degree of sustained distress required to create such a behaviour change is difficult to imagine.

When we look at the statistics it's clear that while the horse has retained a position of great significance despite a current lack of need; in many instances this has come at the cost of good welfare. So much has depended on the horse for so long that our attachment to anthropomorphism is as inevitable as the Trojans drawing that wooden horse into their city. However, let's return to our brief overview of the past 6000 years of domestication as it gives further context to the role of the horse today.

Alexander was great . . .

In the early days of the horse's domestication the equipment used for riding changed very little. Horses were controlled using either a simple leather bit or a loop of rope around the neck. Riding was done bareback or with just a saddle cloth for the rider to sit on. The invention of the bit (in the horse's mouth) occurred at a similar time in human history to the invention of sewing needles, woven cloth, flutes, boats and rope – and 500 years before the invention of the wheel.

It took humans a further two thousand years to invent the saddle and this was done in about 800 BCE by the Sarmatians, a fierce group of nomadic tribes that ranged across the Eurasian Steppe. They were an argumentative sort of people who specialized in war, and their weapons of choice were javelins, lances and bows. The Sarmatian women were just as fierce as the men and fought alongside them. At a recent archaeological dig, the fossilized skeletons of some young Sarmatian teenagers believed to be about thirteen or fourteen years old were found, and both the boys and the girls had noticeably bowed legs — a sign of many hours spent riding. The saddle may very well have been the key to the Sarmatians' success as there are no recorded instances in history in which an army without a saddle ever triumphed over an army with a saddle.

The Sarmatian saddle was quite simple: just two padded leather cushions running either side of the horse's spine and held in place with a girth and quite possibly also a breastplate and a crupper (a strap from the back of the saddle to the underside of the tail). This style of saddle became quite popular and widespread, but it was another 1000 years before the stirrup was invented by the Chinese. This was a significant invention because it allowed a mounted rider to balance better and thus facilitated better accuracy with weapons, and helped riders mount from the ground more easily. Because of stirrups, mounted cavalry became far more effective.

It is possible that stirrups started out as simple loops of rope into which riders placed their big toes. Later, they became more elaborate and structured to accommodate riders from colder climates, who didn't ride with bare feet. Once the stirrup was invented, saddle design had to change in order to prevent horses from getting sore backs from the pressure points of the stirrups, and eventually the first solid tree saddle was invented by the Romans in the first century BCE. (This form of saddle is still most common today: a rigid internal structure made from wood or other materials covered by padding and leather.)

Women and horses

Statistically, horse riding is an unusual past-time. It's one of the most dangerous sports you can participate in. Yet the rest of the world's most dangerous sports are played almost exclusively by men. Horse riding is a statistical anomaly because, in almost all equestrian disciplines, female participants usually out-number men.

The gender disparity in equestrian sports has long been a topic of discussion and the reasons given to explain women's love of horses says more about the way that gender operates in our society than about the truth. 'It's a nurturing sport' or 'It's a social sport' and even 'It's a sport where they get to dress up themselves and their horses'. Maybe the answers are in our history, as answers quite often are. A long time ago, from the sixth century BCE until the first few centuries AD, the Sarmatians roamed around the lands of Russia and Kazakhstan. These mounted nomads were highly skilled horse handlers and fierce warriors.

Sarmatian girls not only dressed like men and hunted, they also rode into battle as soldiers. So fierce were they that

Sarmatian women wouldn't marry until they had killed three enemy soldiers. Interestingly, they were also believed to be the origin of the myth of the Amazons, because it is said that Sarmatian mothers would cauterize the right breasts of their infant daughters so that, when grown, they could draw a bow and throw a javelin unimpeded from the back of a horse.

Nowadays we have sports bras, so some of the Sarmatian habits are somewhat redundant. But despite all that, maybe there's just a little bit of the Sarmatian in those women who choose to ride. I suppose it is possible the Sarmatians were the origin of a warrior woman gene that has spread throughout the world and which draws women to horses still, despite their background or nationality. But I think it's more likely that the Sarmatians — without government or mass forms of communication — simply did a job they had to do, safe from the limitations of gendered expectation. Wherever tribes settled in one spot and lost their nomadic ways, the role of women became more focused on domesticity, their status was eroded and they were more constrained. So for the Sarmatian women the horse was very much a part of their power and independence.

Just as it is now. I think horses offer women power and independence. They offer us the ability to take great risks with our bodies when at every other moment our bodies are under the scrutiny of a society that views them as a commodity. And they offer the opportunity to be assertive without censure

— to control 600 kilograms (94 st) of instinct and muscle. They also offer the possibility of bringing us in touch with some deeper part of ourselves that knows we are capable of absolutely anything. Anything at all. Because for women who love horses, the sound of hooves galloping is loud enough to drown out the voices that constrain us.

Perhaps one of the reasons developments in horse training and equipment were so slow was the lack of communication between various horse-riding communities. While the first known text on horsemanship appeared in about 1345 BCE, it was written on stone tablets, which would have made widespread distribution impossible. Written by Kikkuli, a member of the Hittite tribe, the text outlines exactly how to condition a chariot horse in a period of 214 days. The workload for the Hittites' horses was extreme: they had to march for four weeks and then be able to gallop all day in battle. Kikkuli's method includes faster intervals at the canter once the horses are fit, warm-ups, cool downs, warm water wash-downs, rugs and the feeding of grains. This method has since been reproduced by modern horse trainers with great success.

The next known text about horse training doesn't appear until about 401 BCE and was called *On Horsemanship*. The author, Xenophon (430–357 BCE), was a Greek historian, writer and soldier who wrote prolifically on many subjects. He was a friend of Socrates, the philosopher, and a man of right-wing political tastes who favoured strong leadership in politics but advocated gentleness to horses. Xenophon took part in many battles from the back of a horse, and became a mercenary when democracy was re-established in Athens in 410 BCE.

Amongst Xenophon's many suggestions was that his readers choose a horse with a fleshy back. It's easy to understand his motivation for this when viewed in the context of early Greek clothing. In Xenophon's era underpants had yet to be invented and men wore short (skirted) tunics called chitons, which would have offered very little protection for the more sensitive parts of their anatomy. Xenophon lived prior to the invention of the saddle, so it is easy to see why a horse with a fat-covered back would have been highly prized.

Xenophon was a good example of the revolutionary change in thinking that occurred in Greece from around 600 BCE onwards, in which nature was studied in a rational and objective way. We can thank the Greek school of philosophy for mathematics, physics, musical theory, astronomy, philosophy and also for what we now know as modern science. The famous philosophers Socrates, Plato and Aristotle were all Greeks of that era.

As an interesting aside, Aristotle was the teacher of Alexander the Great, the Macedonian ruler who, riding on his stallion Bucephalus, created an empire that stretched from the Balkans to modern-day Pakistan. Bucephalus, a wild stallion, was given to Alexander when he was twelve. The epitome of an angsty teen, young Alexander defeated the Maedi people when his father left him in charge of the kingdom at age sixteen. When Alexander was nineteen his father, Philip, was stabbed to death by an unhappy male lover and Alexander began his highly successful rampage across pretty much the entire known world. Along the way he founded dozens of cities named Alexandria before dying of malaria in Babylon (now Iraq) at the age of 32.

By the time of Alexander's death in 323 BCE, the history of the horse and the history of humanity were already inextricably linked. Without horses, Alexander's rampage across the known world simply would not have been possible. Conversely, without armies like Alexander's the horse would not have been bred in such large numbers.

And so it went for centuries. The horse carried humans to war and, in return, humans bred the horse in increasingly large numbers. The same is true for almost all fields of human endeavour. Agriculture, transport, building, mining, forestry, hunting, racing and exploration all required horses, and so the numbers of horses grew.

If we allow ourselves to slip, for just a moment, down the rabbit hole of interesting historical asides . . . one of the cities called Alexandria that Alexander the Great founded became the intellectual capital of the world for 800 years. Its massive library housed 700,000 scrolls on which was written all the knowledge of the world. The library's razing by Caliph Omar in 642 CE was both an effective way of brutalizing the population and a way of erasing their past. It's quite likely that some of those 700,000 scrolls would have been dedicated to horse training and management which, as so few texts on horses have survived antiquity, means that the reverberations from an act of war over 1500 years ago can still be felt today. Given the horse's privileged position in ancient society, who knows what insights the ancient texts could have offered us?

Interestingly, Alexandria was also the port city where the Australian and New Zealand soldiers arrived with their horses in 1915, in the early stages of World War I. The effectiveness of the famous Desert Mounted Corps (comprised of the ANZAC Mounted Division, Australian Mounted Division, British Yeomanry, Territorial Horse Artillery and French Cavalry) cannot be refuted. They were an extremely efficient fighting force and were instrumental in ending over 400 years of Ottoman rule in the Middle East.

The tough Waler horses of the Australian Light Horse Brigades often carried over 130 kilograms (20 st) of rider and gear and did it in truly inhospitable conditions, sometimes going over 70 hours without water. And yet, at the end of the war when it was decided it was too expensive (given Australia's stringent quarantine laws) to bring the horses home, they were sold (either to the Indian army or local farmers) or they were euthanized. All horses over the age of twelve had their shoes removed, were shaved of their manes and tails and were shot, and each man was given 7 kilograms of salt to cure his horse's hide with.

Only one of the 136,000 horses that left Australia during World War I returned, and that horse was Sandy, the mount of Major General Sir William Bridges. Sandy returned to Australia via England after Bridges was killed at Gallipoli. Sandy arrived back in Australia in November 1918 and was turned out to pasture at the Central Remount Depot at Maribyrnong. He died in 1923, and his head and neck were stuffed and mounted. For many years visitors to the Australian War Memorial could look at Sandy and perhaps wonder about the 135,999 horses that went to war for Australia and didn't make it home.

General Sir Harry Chauvel was the Australian commander of the Desert Mounted Corps. Harry, as he was known, was a humble man and a wonderful horseperson with a deep understanding of the capabilities and limitations of his men. During the latter half of the campaign in the Middle East he commanded more soldiers on horseback than any other commander in history.

And, to close the loop of interesting historical coincidences, the only other soldier to have commanded a similar sized cavalry was (you guessed it) Alexander the Great.

~

By the start of World War II it was obvious that, as a weapon of war, the horse was being superseded by modern inventions such as the tank. This was becoming a familiar theme in other areas of life as well. Tractors and other mechanized equipment largely replaced horses in agriculture. Cars, motorbikes and trains replaced the horse as a form of transport.

It seemed for a decade or so as though the horse might soon become redundant, and horse numbers began to decline. But the technology that forced the horse's redundancy was also to bring about its renaissance. Thanks to technological advances, for the first time in history humans were faced with an abundance of leisure time. And once again the horse stepped into the breach.

WILHELM

NORTH BERLIN,
1906

Wilhelm looks out at the crowd of people in the stable courtyard. He takes out his pocket watch and squints at the dial. It is nearly noon, just a few minutes until show time.

He brushes a crumb of rye bread from the lapel of his long coat and notices, for the first time, how the cuffs of his best shirt are grey and fraying. Klara would have shaken her head and tutted at him for being untidy but she has been gone five years in June and his housekeeper, Mrs Fischer, is a lazy woman who would rather gossip with the neighbours than starch and mend. At night, when he lies alone in bed, he talks to Klara and in the shadowy evening light her soft-cheeked face smiles back at him from behind the glass of the photo frame.

In the bleak days of her final illness it had been Klara who suggested he buy a horse for company. Wilhelm had grown up with horses and in the 40 years of his marriage to Klara she had listened to him talk for countless hours about hunting foxes across the green fields near Hamburg. How his boots shone like a mirror and every buckle was buffed to gold. He had told her about the family farm and how he had spent many happy days in the paddocks walking beside his grandfather and his team of heavy horses as they dragged neat furrows into the cocoa-coloured soil.

When as a young man he'd moved to the city to start a job as a maths teacher, he had missed his family and the horses so much it almost made him sick. It was meeting Klara that eased the achy day-without-food feeling in his stomach that he got when he thought about home. It was Klara whose shy smile and gentle voice had helped him forget his unhappiness. And so, in the first long days after she died, when he missed her more than he thought was possible, he decided to take her advice and buy a horse.

He first saw the young stallion in an auctioneer's muddy yard. An unbroken youngster, straight from the pasture with a rough coat well seasoned with burrs and dirt. He was unshod and his mane fell in long twisted knots to his shoulder. But still, there was something in the way he held himself. Alert but not frightened, his dark eyes like mahogany, and small, neat ears. Wilhelm reached across the rail and gently stroked the horse's shoulder. 'What a fine fellow you are,' he whispered, and the stallion's head lowered. 'Klara would have liked you. So I will call you Hans for her favourite brother.'

That evening Wilhelm led the horse home through the busy streets of Berlin. 'Steady there, Hans,' he said to the frightened young horse snorting at the end of the lead. 'My knees are sixty years older than yours and my heart can't keep up.' Wilhelm had some crusts of stale bread in his pocket, and when Hans walked quietly or stood to let the trams pass, he would crumble a small piece into his hand and offer it to Hans as a treat. By the time they got to the courtyard Hans was following his new owner quietly and Wilhelm, though tired, felt a small flutter of warmth in his chest, something that he hadn't felt since Klara fell ill. He paused, smoothed the horse's shoulder with his palm — and realized with a smile that what he felt was happiness.

When they were safely in the stable Wilhelm pulled the headcollar over the horse's ears and scratched his neck. 'You are indeed a very special horse,' he said and then laughed. 'To be honest, Klara's brother was kind and a good bootmaker but perhaps not the smartest man ever born. So I will call you Clever

Hans because you are not a suburban bootmaker with a taste for lager. You, my friend, are destined for greater things.'

~

Wilhelm takes out his pocket watch. It is noon, time to start the show.

Clever Hans is tethered in his stall and turns a small, tapered ear towards his owner. Even in the dim light of the stone building Wilhelm can see how the horse's coat is satiny with good health and brushing. 'It's time to show the people just how clever you are, Hans,' says Wilhelm. And he leads the stallion, blinking, into the sunny courtyard.

The crowd grows silent as the man and his horse walk out onto the cobblestones together. They stop next to a large blackboard and Wilhelm pats the large pockets of his coat, feeling for the bread crusts and pieces of carrot he will need for the show. He clears his throat.

'Welcome, ladies, gentlemen and honoured guests,' he begins. 'My name is Herr von Osten and I believe that we gravely underestimate the intelligence of the animals with whom we share our world.

'Before you is my own horse, Clever Hans, a nine-year-old stallion. Today you will see Hans perform feats of calculation, memory and intelligence that many believe impossible. Or have decided are tricks. But there are no tricks here today, ladies and gentlemen.

'Before I begin my display I will point out that just recently an investigating commission of scientists and psychologists has been appointed to study Hans and, while their investigations are ongoing, I can tell you that some of the most respected professors in Berlin have determined that there is no trickery at work in this display. There are no hidden wires or secret signals. Just an old man and an extraordinary horse.

'I knew Hans was clever when I began his training five years ago, but he has again and again surpassed my expectations. I am still surprised and amazed every day by the things he is able to do. Today I will demonstrate just a few of his many, many abilities because to show them all would take a week or even more! You will see him count, tell the time and perform arithmetic. He will recognize people he has met just once, identify painters and composers, name playing cards by suit and coins by denomination. In short, he will truly prove to you that, when trained correctly, horses are not dumb beasts but animals with an intelligence similar to our own. So, without wasting any more time, we shall begin.'

Wilhelm ducks his head towards the crowd and steps towards the chalkboard.

'Hans,' he says in a voice loud enough to be heard by those furthest from the front. 'What is seven multiplied by three?'

The horse lifts a slender foreleg and begins to tap the ground. The crowd is silent. After 21 taps Hans stops tapping and Wilhelm takes a small piece of carrot out of his pocket and feeds it to him.

'What is nine divided by three?'

Hans taps three times. Again Wilhelm gives him a small treat and then turns to the audience.

'When Hans spells, he uses one tap to signify the letter A, two taps for B, three taps for C and so on,' he says and turns back towards the horse. 'Hans, what day of the week is it?'

Hans taps his hoof six times and Wilhelm gives him a treat.

'Luckily for Hans there is only one day of the week that begins with the letter F,' he says to the audience and smiles. 'Now to demonstrate his excellent memory. There is someone in the audience whom Hans met for the first time yesterday. I will ask him now to step forward and we will see if Hans remembers his name.'

A small man in a dark, checked suit steps forward from the audience and stands next to Wilhelm.

'Hans, what is the first letter of this man's surname?'

Hans taps his foot eight times and Wilhelm rewards him with a small piece of bread.

'Sir, could you kindly tell the audience your name?'

The small man clears his throat. 'Hansen. My name is Hansen. Herr Hansen.'

There is a murmur from the audience which gradually grows until the audience is on its feet and clapping. Wilhelm hears 'Bravo, Hans!' from every corner of the courtyard and his heart fills.

When the cheers subside the show continues. A gramophone is brought into the yard. Hans listens to several pieces of music and is able to correctly identify the composers by spelling out their names with his hoof. When asked to identify the colour of a lady's hat he correctly taps out 'blue'. He solves complex maths equations and, when shown reproductions of famous art works, identifies each artist.

After an hour Hans begins to show less interest in the treats. Hearing another horse passing in the street he lifts his head and neighs then shakes his long forelock and stamps a hind foot on the stone floor. Wilhelm strokes his neck and clips a rope to his leather headcollar.

'Ladies, gentlemen and honoured guests, we are now at the end of our display. It is my sincerest hope that you will go away from here today with a renewed appreciation for the intelligence of horses and an improved understanding of their capacity to learn. I thank you for your time and your enthusiasm and hope that the next time you step up into your carriage you will spare a thought for the creature between the shafts.'

After a shallow bow towards the audience Wilhelm quietly turns and leads the young horse from the courtyard back to his stall at the end of the barn. It is quiet in the stable. He packs the manger with straw and fills a metal pail with clean water. The old man watches the horse float his velvety muzzle on the surface of the water and drink with wrinkled lips. He quietly strokes the arch of the horse's neck and allows himself a small smile.

Out in the courtyard, the crowd is leaving. Few people notice a small man in a checked suit leaning against the rough wall, writing on a notepad. No one noticed that he had remained silent while the rest of the crowd cheered, his eyes narrow. As the professor finishes writing his notes, he turns to leave and then pauses, nodding at the darkened doorway of the stable with a small, satisfied smile on his lips.

4.

THE MODERN HORSE

Far from becoming redundant, today there are over 60 million horses on the planet. In the developing world, they are still used for transport, agriculture, meat and milk, though the majority of the world's horse population exists in the developed world, where they are kept mostly for sport and leisure. That the world still has such a robust population of equines speaks volumes about our love for and our connection to the horse.

However, as we will see, that relationship, like the relationships we have with other animal species, is mostly about us.

Let's digress for a moment and take a closer look at how we interact with other species as a way of exploring the anthropocentric mindset that now informs a lot of our interactions with horses. Consider this example. In a recent experiment, researchers were disappointed that their capuchin monkey subjects seemed unable to tell the difference between different human faces — until they decided to test the monkeys' abilities to differentiate between monkey faces. And at this, of course, the monkeys excelled.

I think this experiment says a great deal about humanity's preoccupation with humanity and how our anthropocentric world view informs most of our interactions with the animals in our care. I think it also illustrates very clearly our attachment to our human abilities, an attachment that is so binding that we go looking for our abilities in other species when it would seem more useful and more interesting to look for and celebrate the differences.

~

When it comes our beliefs about the horse, most of us are like laptops already preloaded with software. By the time we're old enough to learn to ride we arrive at the side of the horse complete with the biases and preconceived notions of our generation. And so it has been throughout history as each generation puts its own spin on the characteristics of the horse they deem most important.

In the 21st century the horse is often depicted as kindly and altruistic. Unless of course it is a racehorse, and then it is often described as courageous and deeply competitive. Or a show horse, often described as proud and vain. Or a dressage horse, often described as hard-working and focused. Or a pony club mount, often described as gentle and caring. Or a difficult horse, which could be described as anything from stubborn to crazy. Unsurprisingly, these descriptors have much more to do with our own expectations and preconceived notions than with the horse's behaviour.

In my role as a horse trainer I have heard just about every possible adjective applied to the horse, from depraved to schizophrenic to jealous to lazy and pretty much everything in between. I have yet to meet a horse that is any of those things. This is because the horse's brain is completely different to ours. We have a large and developed prefrontal cortex, the part of the brain dedicated to complex emotional states, planning, deception, cognition and attention. The horse, on the other hand, has a limited prefrontal cortex but a far more developed cerebellum, which means it is far better at movement, balance and interpreting sensory input. The horse is incapable of most of the states we accuse him of simply because he lacks the neurological architecture required to generate them. The frugal diet of a grazer simply does not contain enough macronutrients to run a large, complex and energetically expensive brain.

I suppose on the surface an anthropocentric worldview doesn't seem that destructive. Indeed, it may engender empathy, which is one of our most admirable human traits. But as we will see, if it's allowed to go unchecked, anthropomorphism often leads to poor welfare for the animals in our care.

Language

The field of research viewed by its critics as the most relentlessly anthropomorphic is the quest to teach animals to use human language. However, before we go any further it is useful to deviate slightly and define what we really mean when we use the word language.

Language is not simply a string of words; it is a systematic means of communicating using sounds or symbols. Grammar makes human language infinite — there is no limit to the number of complex sentences that can be constructed. And, as linguist Steven Pinker points out, it is also digital (the infinity is achieved by rearranging discrete elements in particular orders and combinations) and compositional (each of the combinations has a different meaning predictable from the meanings of its parts and the rules and principles arranging them). Consider the three-word example 'shark bites man'. If we rearrange the elements so that it reads 'man bites shark' the meaning is completely different.

Language is so integral to our experience of the world that it is hard for us to imagine a meaningful life without it. When my children were very young, one of the most commonly heard phrases in our house was, 'Use your words, please,' as if to communicate in any other way was somehow less valuable. Indeed, when my youngest son was late to talk, I took him to a specialist to discover the cause. Sitting on my knee in the doctor's office he turned to his older sister, waved his hands and babbled something unintelligible. She turned to me and said, 'He says he'd like a drink now.' The doctor smiled kindly and (perhaps resisting the urge to make a comment about parental anxiety relating to developmental milestones) said, 'He doesn't speak because he doesn't need to.'

I think this is true of the entire animal kingdom. They don't use language because, with their heightened senses and species-specific abilities, they don't need to, in the same way that we don't need the bat's echolocation abilities or the hummingbird's ability to see ultraviolet light and colours we can only dream of. It seems quite likely that language is a unique outcome of our evolution just as echolocation and tetrachromatic vision is for bats and hummingbirds. This is not suggesting that animals do not communicate in nuanced and subtle ways; however, true language with its complex grammar and the possibility of infinite meanings appears to be peculiarly human. But so attached are we to our ability to talk that we've wasted the lives of many innocent animals trying to prove they are lesser versions of ourselves. And because language is so integral to our own experience of the world we tend to forget it has limitations. Imagine trying to explain to an alien what an orange tasted like, or the smell of a baby's head.

Although in the twentieth century there were many examples of humans trying to determine if animals could talk, very few resulted in a positive outcome for the animal. Few examples epitomise this better than Nim Chimpsky.

In the 1970s there was a lot of support (and funding) for scientists studying the acquisition of language by primates. One of the most vocal (pardon the pun) challengers of this area of research was linguist Noam Chomsky, who maintained that language is a uniquely human trait. A team of Columbia University researchers led by Herbert Terrace set out to prove Noam wrong, and they were so confident that in the right environment a chimp could learn to use American Sign Language (ASL) to communicate that they named their research subject Nim Chimpsky as a kind of academic in-joke.

Nim was born in 1973 and taken from his mother at six days of age. He was given to a wealthy American family (with no animal, let alone primate, training experience) to raise as if he was a human infant. He was even breastfed by his surrogate human mother. The family, despite having no experience themselves with ASL, managed to teach Nim 125 different signs. However, by the time he was two years old Nim was deemed too difficult to handle and he was removed from the family and sent to live in a laboratory.

Despite receiving almost full-time training, Nim didn't demonstrate language acquisition in the way the researchers hoped he would. He used signs to acquire food, hugs and other things he wanted (such as the marijuana cigarettes his first family introduced him to) but he never created longer, complex sentences and never used signs for anything other than pragmatic purposes.

When the experiment ended after ten years, Nim was sent to the Institute for Primate Studies in Oklahoma, where for the first time he met other chimps. The institute was a dank, miserable place and prior to Nim's arrival there had been a lot of violence amongst the primate inmates, including three murders and two suicides. It is difficult to imagine how terrifying it must have been for Nim, who had not seen or interacted with another chimp since he was six days old.

Later, he was sold to the Laboratory for Experimental Medicine and Surgery in Primates (LEMSIP) where he was destined to be used in hepatitis vaccine studies. Workers at LEMSIP noticed Nim signing and he was eventually bought by Black Beauty Ranch, an animal rescue centre. Nim lived alone at the sanctuary for several years until he was joined by two other chimps that had also been rescued from LEMSIP.

In his later years Nim became quite aggressive towards humans and violently attacked the woman who raised him when she entered his cage. He also killed a dog. He died from a heart attack at the age of 26, about twenty years short of the average lifespan of a captive chimp.

The documentary made about Nim's sad and troubled life, *Project Nim*, is harrowing viewing and serves as a permanent reminder of the pitfalls of an anthropocentric worldview. As an animal trainer I was deeply troubled by the way Nim was physically punished by his handlers and their absolute lack of any animal training experience. The researchers' expectations that Nim would be able to suddenly integrate into a group of chimps after no exposure between the ages of six days and ten years is so naive it seems disingenuous. Sadly, in the end Nim was little more than collateral damage in an academic difference of opinion.

Wilhelm von Osten and the Clever Hans Effect

There are countless other primates (such as the famous Koko the gorilla) and animals who have lived lesser lives because of the human need to seek out furry, less intelligent versions of ourselves. And the most unsettling aspect of this research is that, decades before the big upswing of interest in animal language acquisition, there was a famous study that elucidated the problems in animal research so clearly that the phenomenon has been named after the research subject.

As we have already learned, in 1906, Wilhelm von Osten, a retired maths teacher, set out to prove horses were smarter than previously believed. He spent four years training his Orlov trotter, Clever Hans, to solve complex mathematical problems and identify composers and artists by their work. Von Osten would ask Hans a question, the horse would begin tapping his hoof and stop when the correct number was arrived at. Clever Hans became famous across Germany and people would travel from far away to watch him demonstrate his amazing capabilities.

Eventually a team of thirteen scientists was given the task of discovering the secret to the horse's incredible mind. Although Hans appeared to be almost supernaturally intelligent, Professor

Oskar Pfungst, one of the team commissioned with investigating the training, noticed the horse would only answer correctly when his owner Wilhelm knew the answer. If von Osten (and later other questioners) didn't know the answer, or if they were hidden from the horse's sight, he started to make errors. Pfungst noticed that, when questioned, the horse would begin tapping and, without meaning to or even knowing that he was doing it, von Osten would subtly change his posture when the correct number was reached. Because of classical conditioning Hans had paired the slight postural change with the treat and thus stopped tapping.

Von Osten truly believed his horse could count and was heartbroken when it became clear that he couldn't. He died in 1909, a bitter and disappointed man. In 1914 when World War I broke out Clever Hans, who in his previous life had never been ridden or driven in harness, was drafted into the army and was one of many millions of horses killed during the war. It is believed he was killed by gunfire in 1916 and his body eaten by starving soldiers.

The Clever Hans Effect, as it has come to be known, highlights that animal researchers should avoid face-to-face contact during scientific trials to prevent their animal subjects from interpreting miniscule changes in body language or facial expression. Although the Clever Hans Effect has been known about since the beginning of the twentieth century it seems that, in the world of animal research at least, those who cannot remember the past are condemned to repeat it.

Natural horsemanship, and the dominance and submission paradigm

By the 1960s the sport of equestrian was really starting to take off. Dressage, showjumping and eventing became increasingly more popular, and in the horse-breeding areas of the world, the heavy horses that had once been so vital for agriculture were bred with lighter, finer breeds to create modern horses more suitable for equestrian sport than ploughing or pulling a cart.

Alongside these newer types of horse came a desire to renegotiate the relationship between our species. The older ways of training and managing horses were perceived by many as overly harsh and did not fit with the horse's new role. At the same time, there was an increase of scientific interest in equine ethology (the study of horses in their natural environment). In the 1980s the desire to modify existing training practices coalesced with the emerging body of literature on ethology and morphed into a way of training and thinking about horses that eventually became known as natural horsemanship.

Natural horsemen and women were the icebreakers for change. They applied science where previously there was only tradition. By doing so they bore the brunt of old school scepticism, and while a lot of their methods have since been abandoned, their work paved the way for positive change and a more welfare-friendly approach to horse training.

The rise of the natural horsemanship movement marked a definite departure from the Clever Hans/Nim Chimpsky philosophy of interspecies communication. Instead of attempting to teach the horse human language, the natural horseman attempted to co-opt the horse's own communication strategies and herd dynamics and use them in training. While the belief that humans can somehow mimic horse communication signals is flawed for various reasons that we will discuss later, one of the most problematic spin-offs of this new style of training was a philosophy that also became popular amongst dog trainers, and which has since come to be known as the dominance and submission paradigm.

The dominance and submission school of training stems from the (mistaken) idea that herd animals will submit to an animal that is above them in the pecking order. Despite enjoying a period of popularity, this belief does not stand up to any more than cursory scientific scrutiny. Indeed, I often think of it as the animal trainer's version of 'broscience', the term used to describe the misconceptions and ideas of questionable scientific credibility circulated in the fitness industry. When applied to horse training, I like to call the dominance and submission paradigm 'hoscience'.

The dominance and submission paradigm asserts that to train the horse, the human should take the position of the alpha animal. This notion demonstrates a very flawed way of thinking about herd structure. Within the herd, hierarchy is not arranged like ranks in the military, but rather ebbs and flows depending on the context. The social signals used to maintain order can be so subtle that observers can often find it difficult to determine which horse is dominant at any time. A reductionist (dominance and submission) view of herd hierarchy fails to acknowledge the complex and rich social lives of the animals within the herd, whose interactions are far more nuanced and intricate than the term 'pecking order' would suggest. Horses have bilateral dominance, which means they know their own relationship to other horses but don't have an overarching mental framework for the social structure of the herd.

By way of illustration, most of the gestures horses use to communicate with each other are so fleeting and subtle that to see them we need to film them and watch them in slow motion. The horse, with her large cerebellum, is exquisitely sensitive to tactile and visual cues while we, compliments of our large prefrontal cortex, are great at planning, imagining and overthinking.

The physical structures the horse uses to communicate with other horses include four legs, a long flexible neck, mobile ears, side-mounted eyes, a long tail and large nostrils. Compared to the horse we have squinty, front-facing eyes that constantly show their whites, miniscule nostrils, a two-leg deficit, tiny fixed ears, a short immobile neck and a total lack of tail. How utterly human to believe we could possibly mimic the horse's beautifully tailored communication system, developed over millions of years of evolution and so subtle our vision mostly cannot even see it.

Unfortunately, the dominance and submission paradigm has been used as a justification for some of the most brutal and pointless training strategies I've ever seen. In the quest to achieve dominance I've heard of trainers tying up horses for excessively long periods of time, tripping them over and chasing them to the point of exhaustion. It goes without saying that none of these strategies has any place in an ethical training system. Luckily the notion of dominance has largely fallen by the wayside in mainstream horse training but sadly it is, I believe, enjoying a bit of a resurgence amongst some dog trainers. Moves like the 'alpha roll' are vestiges of this belief system, and most ethical dog trainers I have spoken to argue that, at best, they are pointless and, at worst, terrifying and emotionally damaging for the dog.

From the school of dominance and submission arose the notion that, to be trained, the horse should respect the trainer. Respect is a word that carries a very hefty freight of meaning in most cultures and is quite often accompanied by no small amount of fear. Another version of ethological hoscience, the idea of respect is somewhat flawed when dealing with an animal with almost no prefrontal cortex. How do you increase the horse's respect for the trainer if the training fails? This is a question that has, sadly, often been answered in the past with excessive and/or painful force.

When training the dogs and horses with which we share our lives it's easy to slip into anthropomorphic thought patterns. I have been lucky enough to be a training consultant for a wide range of animal species and, in my experience, non-domesticated animals have a wonderful way of helping you decide what is relevant in a training context and what is not. In Darwin, in northern Australia, I saw a magnificent 3-metre (10 ft) saltwater crocodile trained to swim to a target. It is easy for the trainers to respect this beautiful reptile — its sheer presence is daunting, even from the other side of a strong fence. But it's not a two-way street. The crocodile doesn't respect his trainers; indeed, if any of them fell into his enclosure he would view them simply as prey, as 55 kilograms of conveniently slow, thin-skinned beef.

It may seem disingenuous to point this out, but what the school of dominance and submission and the trainers seeking respect fail to acknowledge is that the horse has eyes. The horse can clearly tell the difference between itself and a human, and ham-fisted analogues of equine communication signals are not going to fool it into believing otherwise. It would be maladaptive for a prey species to adopt another species into its herd, just as it would be maladaptive for a horse to be chased into showing another species respect.

The horse has been a horse for 55 million years and at no time has it ever asked to be trained. We domesticated the horse, and its welfare is our responsibility. If the horse makes mistakes during training it is not the horse's fault. It is not a lack of respect or the act of social climbing, but the fault of the human who is holding the reins.

For me, it is an enormous privilege to sit astride a young horse as it takes its first tentative steps under saddle. That moment connects me to the long line of humans throughout history who have nurtured this extraordinary bond between our species. The horse improves us. We can jump higher and run faster and further on the back of a horse. We are more graceful. We are braver. But more than that, the horse offers us a chance to be the best version of ourselves. Kinder, more consistent, more patient. And that, perhaps, is the greatest gift that any being could bestow upon another.

Attachment theory

If the relationship between horses and humans cannot be described as based on herd dynamics, or respect or dominance, how can we describe it? Many animal behaviourists and an increasingly large body of scientific literature are pointing towards a form of attachment.

Attachment theory, which explains the bonds between humans, was first documented by John Bowlby and Mary Ainsworth. Bowlby described it as a 'lasting psychological connectedness between human beings'. The underlying premise of attachment theory is that human infants are programmed by evolution to maintain a close connection with their primary caregivers.

Attachment theory arose in almost direct opposition to a philosophy that was spreading throughout the western world regarding the raising of children. In the early twentieth century there was an excruciatingly high mortality rate of babies in orphanages and children's hospitals. When it was eventually discovered that germs and bacteria spread disease, these homes were cleaned to the point of obsessiveness. And as a way of further stopping the spread of disease the nurses and caretakers were forbidden to handle the children more than was absolutely necessary. At the same time as this was developing, behaviourists Watson and Skinner were proposing that babies only become attached to their mothers because the mothers give them milk. Infants, they theorized, needed little more than food, shelter and cleanliness in order to thrive.

And yet the babies in orphanages continued to die.

In the 1960s American psychologist Harry Harlow published a paper that would not only prove the behaviourists wrong but would also save the lives of countless children. In Harlow's now famous experiments, baby rhesus monkeys were taken from their mothers and placed in a cage with two model 'mothers'. One, made from wire, contained the monkey's bottle of milk. The other contained no milk but was covered with soft fluffy fabric. Although the baby monkeys would feed readily from the wire mother they showed no attachment to it, and when startled would cling to the cloth mother for comfort. Harlow showed that comfort and security is enormously important to babies — so important, in fact, that they will die without it.

It's easy to see, then, how Bowlby and Ainsworth's work on attachment theory in babies was quite revolutionary for its time. It wasn't very many decades prior to its publication that the world had supposed that human babies were better off without cuddling and overt displays of love and affection. Attachment theory not only suggests that the opposite is true, it also theorizes that the ways babies attach to their caregivers can affect the way they love for the rest of their lives. Attachment theory is now used as a way of describing romantic relationships and it has been shown that dysfunctions in an adult's attachment style can result in problems in long-term relationships.

More recently, attachment theory has also been used to explain the bonds between humans and their pets. Mostly it has been used to explain the close attachment humans feel for animals, but it is not too large a leap of faith to suggest that the bond animals have with their caregivers could also be explained by attachment theory. Most of the domestic animals with whom we share our lives are mammals, which means they have a fairly long period of time, from birth to weaning, when they are totally dependent on their mother. It is possible that attachment, a hardwired behaviour that bonds baby to mother, lies at the heart of our relationship with animals and theirs with us.

Although there are undoubtedly genetic differences that predispose attachment, there seems to be several conditions under which attachment is optimal. The first is that the caregiver must offer a place of perceived safety. This is not only physical but also emotional safety; the caregiver must be reliable and predictable. Secondly it is important that the caregiver meets the needs of the baby (or dog/horse, etc.) by providing food and shelter. Third, the caregiver must be able to offer comfort in times of distress.

Most people will understand how a loved pet can provide comfort. When I was a teenager I remember very clearly how good it felt to come home from school and hug my dog. On stressful days now I yearn to hug my partner and can't wait to see him after work. I also find comfort amongst my horses and goats (although I would never tell my partner that he has been partially usurped by Colin, an 80-kg/12½ st Saanen wether). I believe the attachment works both ways, because my bottle-reared goats will call to me when something frightens them, even though now they significantly outweigh me. I provide them with the perception of safety just as they provide me with comfort.

Attachment isn't just good for us mentally, it also has many physical benefits and there are countless studies showing the many health advantages of pet ownership. But interestingly there are health benefits for animals too. In a long study of the effect of a high-fat diet on cholesterol in rabbits, researchers were confused as to why one group of bunnies had a 60 per cent reduction in arterial clogging. After examining all the data and variables they discovered that the lab assistant responsible for the less clogged rabbits spent a fair proportion of every day cuddling, grooming and just generally loving her charges. They were astounded but, more importantly, were able to replicate the results with another group of rabbits.

It's not possible to say if the bunnies were attached to their caregiver in the true sense of Bowlby and Ainsworth's model, but nevertheless, the implications are both astounding and yet unsurprising. Feeling loved makes us happier and healthier. It's no surprise that feeling loved does the same thing for animals.

TED

EXCERPT FROM THE DIARY OF TROOPER EDWARD THOMPSON, ANZAC MOUNTED DIVISION

31 December 1915

Well, it's New Year's Eve in Cairo and here I am. I never thought I'd be the sort to keep a diary, but then again, I never thought I'd sail halfway round the world to shoot at some fellas I'd never met. Funny, isn't it, how things change?

Thankfully my wound is healing well, just a bit of bark off my shoulder now the shrapnel's out. Bloody Gallipoli. We left far too many good men on that blasted bit of country and if I hadn't been bent over tying my bootlace when the shell burst, one of them would have been me. But I was lucky, by the time we berthed in Alexandria I could walk off the ship myself and after a couple of weeks in a hospital bed I was chafing to get back to camp. I beat the rest of the boys in my section back to Egypt by a few weeks and, lucky for me, got the first pick at the horse lines.

There are some nice horses over here but I got the best I reckon. He's only about seven and not tall, maybe fifteen hands, but he's so close coupled he feels like a coiled spring to ride and he's as brave as they come. If you were going to fault him you'd say he was maybe a bit short in the rein and heavy with it, but he's a Waler and that draft blood will tell in the end. Good straight legs and feet as close to perfect as you can get. When I put his first set of shoes on it was just a pleasure to put the steel under him.

Whenever I can pinch a bit of sugar for him from the mess he follows me around the camp like a sheep dog. So I've called him Cobber because he's my friend. He's an absolute pearler and just the sort of horse Dad would like. The sergeant at the horse lines said they'd been planning on saving him for one of the brass, but the poor fellow copped it on the beach a week before we withdrew.

Things are pretty slow at the moment. Mostly we're just sorting out horses and gear and filling up the gaps in each section with new fellas fresh off the boat. The tucker is terrible but it's not cold and our bell tents are pretty comfortable. They say the Turks are going to try to take the Suez Canal. I say let them try. We're mounted now and without those damn Gallipoli hills to give them cover the Turks are going to have their work cut out for them. Some of the boys are saying we'll have this whole thing wrapped up by Christmas. Well, wouldn't that be grand.

I miss home something terrible. Dad most of all, but I miss the trees and the green hills too. Here it's just flat and brown as far as the eye can see. Scorpions the size of mud crabs and so many flies — I no longer count how many of the blighters I eat with every meal.

Some nights I dream we're mustering and I'm in my swag by a waterhole. I can hear magpies singing the dawn chorus and the first light is coming through the trees. Dad's got the fire going and the billy on, I can hear the chink of hobble chains and the stamp of the heifers grazing nearby. And then one of the boys coughs and I wake up and I'm in a tent in Egypt wishing I was home.

10 August 1916

Today was a good day. The mail came and Dad had sent a package. The biscuits tasted just like home and they weren't at all stale, even though it took them five months to get here! When I told the boys Dad cooked them himself, they couldn't believe it. Then I told them he can also knock up a roast dinner and a ripper sponge cake, too, if the hens are laying. I'm pretty sure they thought I was lying. Compared to Dad's cooking, the food over here is awful but there's plenty of it, in fact I think I've grown (at the ripe old age of nineteen). Well, either that or my sleeves have shrunk.

In the past months we've had no time to get bored, in fact we've had little time for rest. Cobber is game for absolutely anything, I don't think I've ever ridden a horse with so much heart. The little fella looks like a thoroughbred now — all sinew and muscle and if he's tired you wouldn't know it. When the whole division's mounted up and there's row upon row of Walers with their coats shining in the sun, it's a heart-stirring sight. Makes me proud to be a light horseman.

Last week we faced our toughest test since we got back from the Dardanelles, and it just reinforced what a formidable force we are when mounted. The Turks have been sneaking their way down through Palestine for months, heading for the canal. The brass must have figured out they'd come past Romani so for the past few weeks that's where we've been, camped out in the desert on reduced water rations. It's so damn hot out here you can barely breathe. The poor horses get just a few pints of water a day and some dusty barley straw that the locals call tibbin. It's so tough, it's unbelievable.

Last week we dug in a couple of miles from the base of some big hills. There were no Turks in sight but we do what we're told. A couple of days went past and then, in the middle of the night, we hear this bloody awful screaming as thousands of Turks attacked. They yelled, 'Allah! Allah! Finish Australia!' as they charged and though it sounds kind of funny in their accent, it still puts the wind up you. We shot them at point-blank range, just like shooting fish in a barrel as Uncle Frank used to say. In our section alone at least 50 dead men piled up just in front of our trench. But they kept coming and the order came to withdraw slowly, fighting all the way. I was horse handler, so I kept Cobber and the three other horses calm — they're so brave, the noise is unbelievable what with artillery and gunfire. All day long we fought them and into the night. We slept in the sand and we were back into it by dawn the next morning.

It's strange, when you're in the thick of it you don't always know what's going on, it's just shelling and bullets and keep your head down. It's as if you're a part of a giant puppet show and someone else is pulling the strings. And then something happens and you realize that what seemed like absolute chaos was actually part of a plan. That's how it was at Romani. Eventually, at the base of a big ridge, we were ordered to hold our line. The second and third brigades had been waiting, out of sight, and they attacked the Turks from the flanks, boxing them in. Then, just when Jacko thought it couldn't get any worse, the artillery started, raining down so much lead that the sand turned red. By the end of that day there were 5000 dead Turks on the battlefield.

But that wasn't the end of it. What was left of the Turkish army withdrew, back across the desert — and after feeding and watering the horses we were given the order to chase them. They tried to stand their ground at Katia because that's the last water for miles, but we were too strong for them and they bolted. So here we are, camped in the desert wondering what the brass have got planned for us next.

The seasons in this bloody country are all arse about, so it's summer here while it's winter at home. It's hard to wrap your head around that. I never planned on being gone this long and I worry about Dad trying to run the farm on his own. I mean, he isn't getting any younger. I tell myself that Mum is watching over us both and I know that she'd be proud. I keep picturing myself waking up in my own bed, looking out the window and seeing Cobber grazing. After all this bloody sand he's going to love the hinterland.

1 May 1917

Another good day. We got mail and, as well as a letter from Dad, Aunt Catherine sent socks. They're always very much appreciated as the nights here are hellishly cold. In the middle of the night it's cold enough to give you chilblains but by morning smoko you could cook an egg on the sand.

I'm here to do a job, but I can tell you, if it was up to me I wouldn't waste my time fighting over this country. Sand, sand and more bloody sand. And don't forget the flies. You'd be hard pressed to make one decent farm out of the whole bloody place. There's a tribe called the Bedouin. They live on the outskirts, follow the fighting and steal anything they can, including the boots and uniforms off dead soldiers. Even if it's Jacko that they're stealing off, that sort of thing really winds me up.

We've been chasing the Turks all over the Sinai for months now. They held us off at Gaza twice, after some pretty tough fighting. We'd have had them the second time around but the blokes in charge pulled us out before we could get the job done. Pretty frustrating really. But you learn something every time you face the enemy and we're only getting stronger as a fighting force.

Cobber is superb, there's just no other way to describe him. As tough as any horse I've ever met and yet he comes to a whistle and will take sugar out of my hand as gently as a lap dog. He'll go all day on a couple of pints of water and a handful of tibbin then lay down beside me on the sand to sleep. He's never let me down and I can't say that about too many people except for Mum and Dad.

The Walers will win the war for us, I reckon. The weedy little Bedouin horses are fast and tough but the Walers are faster and tougher. They're in a class of their own. At Romani as we were retreating, a few Anzacs got separated from their horses and left behind. Major Shanahan went back, picked them up, then galloped nearly a mile with a man in front, a man behind and a man hanging onto each stirrup. Five men on one horse, that's bloody amazing.

There's talk of us getting some leave pretty soon, somewhere out by the coast. What a treat that will be. Swimming in the sea and a chance for the horses to put on a bit of condition. I still remember the first time I saw the sea. Dad took me to Brisbane, I must have been about ten. I'd never seen anything as big as that ocean, the waves looked enormous. A good memory.

15 November 1917

To say we've had a busy few weeks would be a bloody understatement. After the stuff-ups at Gaza we felt like we had to save a bit of pride and we've done all that and more in the last month.

The Turks have built a bloody great line of trenches and redoubts between Gaza and a pissant town called Beersheba to bottleneck the way into Palestine. This war is all about water and Beersheba has good wells, which they reckon were built by Abraham from the Bible. I was never much interested in Bible stories but I believe he was a fella who toured around the desert a fair bit so he obviously understood the value of a good well. Anyway, nowadays Beersheba is a camel-trading town with absolutely nothing to recommend it but the water.

The Turks were dug in like wombats at Beersheba and we hadn't managed to shift them from Gaza so that defensive line was looking pretty bloody solid. Anyway, one afternoon word came down the line that there was a big push on and we're to saddle up. We rode through that night and the next. Bull dust like I've never seen, bugger-all water for the horses and stinking hot.

By the time we got to Beersheba the battle was going full tilt, artillery and infantry going at it hammer and tongs. It went like that all day without much progress and meanwhile the horses were getting thirstier and there was no water, except in the town. We were shitting bricks because we'd worked out that half the horses wouldn't make it back to the camp near Gaza if they didn't get water. We needed to take that town.

It was starting to get close to dusk and we were staring down the barrel of another night without water when we were told to saddle up. We lined up about two miles from town with the boys from the twelfth, 800 or so light horsemen all in a row. The approach to Beersheba is a long, downhill stretch and we started off at a trot, then a canter. You don't really hear that many hoofbeats on the ground, you feel it in your chest. It's something I'll never forget.

We were given the order to charge and we spurred the horses on. Straight at the Turkish trenches and we could see the flash of muzzle fire, but the horses were fighting for their heads, they could smell the wells I reckon. I was knee to knee with the blokes either side of me, bayonets fixed and everyone was yelling and the gunfire and artillery were as loud as anything I've ever heard.

The Turks were waiting for us to dismount and fight like usual, but we'd been given the order to gallop all the way to the town centre and by the time they realized we weren't stopping it was too late for them to change their rifle sites. I could feel the bullets going over our heads but I was scrubbing Cobber's neck like we were coming up the home straight at the races. I could see the trenches coming up and I had no plan but I knew that Cobber would do the best that he could.

We got to the first line and bugger me if Cobber didn't sail straight over it like a bloody steeplechaser. I saw the faces of the Turks flash past beneath us and then we were onto the next line and he took that like a champion too. We galloped straight into the centre of town where about 150 of us were able to stop a mob of sneaky Turkish bastards from blowing up the wells.

We took a big load of prisoners that afternoon, which we had to look after, but I'll be buggered if I'll let a Turk drink before my horse has had his fill. It seems that some of the Turkish brass were living pretty high on the hog in Beersheba, because the next day we found a lot of fancy wine called cognac and some weird tins of food that we ate even though we couldn't read the labels. Made me a bit crook in the guts to be honest, but I'm all right now.

They got us together the next day and told us we'd made history. Not sure about that but I know I'll remember that charge for the rest of my life. Another thing I know is that I was sitting on the best horse I'm ever likely to sit on.

Anyway, we're pushing ahead now that we've smashed the Turkish line and there's a rumour that it'll be Jerusalem next.

5.

THE CONSCIOUS HORSE

It seems to me that as the world changes and science progresses we need to constantly renegotiate the relationships we have to things that once upon a time seemed fixed and immutable. We have changed our relationship to things like climate, biological sex, gender and race to such a degree that the old beliefs seem at the very least antiquated, if not barbaric. Although, for some, change can be confronting, I think it's always worth remembering that the *Slavery Abolition Act* was passed throughout the British Colonies in 1833, less than 200 years ago. And now, what once seemed like an act of revolution is merely a 'how were we ever that brutal?' footnote in the history books.

In the 17th century Galileo was threatened with torture by the Inquisition for his denial of the (Catholic) belief that the world was the stationary centre of the universe, yet he apparently muttered the eloquent denial, 'Eppur si muove' or 'And yet it moves'. And though we now know that the sun and the planets do not revolve around Earth, it seems to me there is still a strong belief that life on this planet revolves around us. Our absolute dominion over animals and the anthropomorphism at the heart of our interactions with them position us at the centre. It's almost as though we can't completely dispel the notion that humans and human activity are the pivot around which the world turns. But perhaps that view will change over time and maybe, in the future, rather than see ourselves as the rightful overlords of the world we inhabit, we will come to see ourselves simply as fellow travellers on the road of life.

Consciousness, sentience and sapience

One of the most significant first steps towards the renegotiation of our relationship with animals occurred in 2012 and it centred on the concept of consciousness in animals. We'll discuss the Cambridge Declaration on Consciousness in more detail later, but before we do, it's important to understand a little bit more about the complexities of consciousness in animals, because while consciousness is relatively straightforward to define, it's far harder to determine why it exists.

To be conscious is to be able to have some kind of subjective experience or awareness. As conscious beings we can experience both external and internal events. We have subjective views on and perceptions of the world and our own bodies. These perceptions include vision, sounds, odours, tastes and tactile experiences. And although we are certain we possess consciousness, we still have no true understanding of where in the brain it originates and how it is produced. Or, as philosopher Colin McGinn put it, we have no idea 'how tech our phenomenology arises from grey soggy matter'.

And if human consciousness is both hard to define and difficult to fully understand, the concept of animal consciousness is even more problematic. One of the most pressing questions facing ethicists and philosophers now is: to what degree do individual animal species possess consciousness?

One of the challenges with determining the extent of an animal's consciousness is that we can't discuss it with the animal in question and compare notes. We have to make best guesses based on observations. And, given our anthropocentric tendencies and history of global domination (not to mention the significant conflict of interest involved with the billions of factory-farmed animals we have, in many instances, condemned to a miserable existence), it's really hard to make objective decisions. But morally the need to answer this question is imperative because it will shape the ways in which we manage animal populations in the future.

When consciousness includes an ability to discriminate between positive and negative perceptual experiences, it becomes sentience. Sentient beings have interests. Imagine a computer system that can perceive the outside world. Regardless of how sensitive the computer's digital senses are or how complex its software, it would still lack the capacity to have either positive or negative experiences. It wouldn't care if it continued to exist but it would be able to perceive the outside world, so it would be conscious. However, if somehow the computer was able to take pleasure in aspects of its existence, to fear its own death or to be pleased about the prospect of continuing to exist, it would have become sentient.

When sentience includes self-awareness it becomes sapience. Sapient creatures have the ability to think and to recognize themselves as individuals. They recognize themselves as beings separate from the environment and the rest of their kind. While sentience is primarily concerned with feelings, sapience is primarily concerned with thinking (or cognition).

The problem is that, for many theorists, sentience and sapience are reliant on language. Language structures our human experience of reality and it's hard to imagine life without it. But, as we've already discussed, isn't language just a purely human trait in the same way that a bat's echolocation skills are a purely bat trait? If the shoe was on the other foot (or wing) and we swapped language for echolocation, wouldn't it be impossible for us to imagine life without echolocation? Wouldn't we view creatures without echolocation as somehow less sentient than us?

The same applies to the search for consciousness-producing structures in animal brains, which has in the past had a fairly anthropocentric focus. It has been theorized that if it was possible to identify the structures within the human brain that produce consciousness researchers could then identify those same structures within animals' brains and could use that to determine the extent to which consciousness exists in each species. However, the 'grey soggy matter' (both ours and animals') remains unforthcoming and the search for consciousness-producing structures continues.

It has long been believed that sentience was impossible without a centralized nervous system, because this is the biological system that produces human consciousness. However, over the past couple of decades this belief has been called into question thanks, in part, to the wonderfully dextrous octopus.

All vertebrate brains share the same basic architecture, in the same way that most houses possess walls, doors and a roof. This basic structure was bequeathed to us by a common ancestor (which is also why all mammals share a certain percentage of their DNA). The common ancestor we share with the octopus is so ancient that the evolutionary path we share diverged at least 600 million years ago. Which is extraordinary because it means, as neurologist Peter Godfrey-Smith points out, that evolution built sentience at least twice.

The soft-bodied, eight-limbed octopus has some extraordinary cognitive abilities. Octopuses use tools and will often carry around two coconut or clam shells to reassemble for later use as a shelter from predators. Tool use, for a long time considered a peculiarly human capability, has been documented in a wide number of species, including birds, primates and bottlenose dolphins (who have been recorded carrying around sponges to assist with foraging).

The octopus will change colour to blend in with its surroundings, taking on the colour of the coral or rock. It has both short- and long-term memory, it plays, it sleeps. It is curious about novel objects. It can recognize human faces. Octopuses can navigate through mazes and are adept at escape behaviour. Indeed, in one laboratory the octopus subjects learned to escape their tanks at night, break into other tanks and eat the crustacean occupants. Researchers couldn't work out why their crayfish numbers were declining because the octopuses left no trace of their midnight snackery, even replacing the tank lids once they'd climbed out. When motion sensor lights were set up to deter them, they learned to extinguish the lights in their tanks by squirting water at the bulbs until they short-circuited. This became so expensive that the octopuses had to be released back into the sea.

And yet the brain of the octopus is totally and utterly unlike ours. It is difficult to say where the brain of the octopus begins and ends. Most of the brain-like neurons are in its arms and it can taste with its feet but, despite the lack of similarity, it too generates both consciousness and sentience. The octopus demonstrates not only that consciousness is complex, nuanced and multifaceted, but also that a mammalian brain is not a prerequisite.

(What is the plural of octopus? There are three ways to talk about more than one octopus and they are all correct: octopi, octopuses and octopodes.)

It's easy to see how the 2012 Cambridge Declaration on Consciousness, made by a group of respected scientists in the field of cognition, was revolutionary. Human consciousness has yet to be fully understood and yet this document declares that many animal species display behaviours complex enough to infer consciousness. The declaration reads:

> *The absence of a neocortex does not appear to preclude an organism from experiencing affective states. Convergent evidence indicates that non-human animals have the neuroanatomical, neurochemical, and neurophysiological substrates of conscious states along with the capacity to exhibit intentional behaviours. Consequently, the weight of evidence indicates that humans are not unique in possessing the neurological substrates that generate consciousness. Non-human animals, including all mammals and birds, and many other creatures, including octopuses, also possess these neurological substrates.*

The scientists involved in writing the declaration cited evidence that found emotions are not confined only to the prefrontal cortex. Bird cognition, for example, seems to arise from structures very similar to that responsible for mammalian cognition. And animals get stoned in similar ways to people.

In the years since 2012 the study of animal consciousness has drawn together researchers from fields as varied as animal welfare, cognitive neuroscience, comparative psychology, philosophy and evolutionary biology to answer the age-old question of animal consciousness. And still no definitive answers exist.

It appears that cognition and consciousness are inextricably linked. But how do we determine an animal's cognitive abilities except in an anthropomorphic way? Animals have such a mind-boggling array of different capabilities that might be instinctive but might also be cognitive. How do we know? How can we tell the difference between instinct and cognitive ability? For example, dung beetles that possess a sesame-seed-sized brain can navigate by the moon and on cloudy nights they navigate using the wind. Which is pretty amazing. Sharks find prey using their ability to detect electrical fields, using small mucus-filled pores on their snouts called the Ampullae of Lorenzini. Which is also amazing. However, both are almost certainly instinctive behaviours. (Speaking of sharks, some species, including great whites, blue, thresher and leopard sharks are oviviparous, which means the eggs hatch in their mother's oviduct. Usually the strongest baby sharks will eat almost all their brothers and sisters before they are born. A fun game I like to play at family gatherings is to look at my children and try to decide, if they were sharks, which one would have eaten the other two.)

But back to trying to determine if an ability is instinctive or cognitive . . . Ravens plan ahead when offered tools that they will need later for a task they would never encounter in the wild. The same ravens fashion wire into hooks so they can obtain out-of-reach food rewards, and place rocks into water to float food to within beak-grasping distance.

If giraffes are given two transparent containers, one filled mostly with slices of their favourite food (carrots) and another with slices of a less loved food (courgettes), and a handler reaches one hand into each container and offers the giraffe slices from each with closed hands, the giraffe will choose the hand that reached into the carrot container each time.

Crows in Japan use cars to break open nuts that are too hard for their beaks. But they don't just drop them on the road — they drop them onto pedestrian crossings so that they can safely retrieve the nuts once the cars stop. It's difficult to explain this as instinct. Young chimpanzees, meanwhile, easily outperform university students in tests of working memory.

When zebra finches sleep they dream of singing, their brains firing in exactly the same patterns as when they are awake and singing the complex songs they learn from other, older finches. Their dreams help them to consolidate the songs they learned during the day, but sometimes they dream new songs that then become part of their daytime repertoire.

As more is learned about the cognitive abilities of animals and how this impacts consciousness, it has become more and more apparent that consciousness is not as simple as a switch that's either on or off. Neither is it as straightforward as a continuum scale or a spectrum with 'not conscious' at one end and 'conscious' at the other. It's much more a multidimensional process as variable and complex as the animals themselves.

Most researchers are happy to agree that the horse is both conscious and sentient. This is, of course, something that those of us who live and work amongst them have always believed. Scratch an itchy horse and they will stretch out their top lip with enjoyment and manoeuvre their body to get your hand to exactly the right place. Gently stroke the neck of a horse and most of the time, if you continue long enough, they will lower their head and sleepily close their eyes. These moments quite clearly have a positive valence which is easy to prove, because if you scratch a horse straight after a behaviour, the incidence of that behaviour will increase. This means that the scratching and/or stroking is reinforcing which, in turn, means it must be pleasant for the horse.

The reverse is true for situations with a negative valence. After receiving a shock, horses will avoid with great care any fence that appears to be electric. Sensitive horses often show distress when the girth is tightened, or expand their ribcage so that once the rider has put the saddle on and tightened the girth, the horse can relax their ribs and the girth will be looser. This behaviour is usually called 'blowing out' and several decades ago when I was learning to ride I was told to knee or elbow the horse sharply in the ribs in order to surprise it into relaxing enough so the girth could be tightened. If I am ever despondent about the glacial rate at which positive change for welfare occurs, I just remember the 'old days' and I'm thankful that we have come so far.

The five criteria for sentience

The concept of sentience is complex and, rather than viewing it as a binary process, it's useful to see it as an interlocking web of cognitive and physiological abilities. It has recently been proposed by researchers in this field that consciousness should be assessed over at least five criteria: perceptual richness, evaluative richness, unity, temporality and self-consciousness. Let's look at each of these in greater detail.

Perceptual richness

This is all about the acuity of an animal's senses and, as a prey species that evolved to avoid being another creature's lunch, the horse's perceptual world is wonderfully rich.

When discussing the horse's perceptual abilities, we often compare them to our own because this is the only perspective we have. However, it's important not to view ours as the gold standard or some kind of perceptual benchmark. Indeed, given the limitations of language, I think it's quite possible that horses (and other animals) have sensory abilities for which we simply do not have the words. Right now, we have an understanding of the abilities we share with the animal kingdom (because we can describe them) but it's quite likely there are many more yet to discover.

Let's begin by looking at equine vision, a sense so completely different to ours that it is difficult to imagine what the world looks like for a horse. The horse's eyes are eight times larger than ours and located on the side of the head, which makes the horse very difficult to sneak up on.

Horses have two kinds of vision. When they use monocular vision their eyes work separately, which allows them to constantly scan their environment for danger. Each eye sees an arc of about 200 degrees, giving the horse a very wide visual range. Horses can also use both eyes together. This is called binocular vision. It allows for focus and depth perception and has a visual range of about 80 degrees. Even when using their panoramic monocular vision, horses still have two blind spots of about 20 degrees each, one directly in front of the nose and one directly behind the rump, both extending out for a couple of metres. It is because of the backwards-facing blind spot that beginner riders are always cautioned not to approach horses from behind. Horses are quite likely to be surprised by a human appearing out of the void and kick out.

For the past few million years, horses have been relatively big and heavy, and therefore there was no need for their vision to adapt for avoiding aerial predators. Unlike humans, who have a round area of cone cells in the eye called the fovea centralis (which gives us our sharp, central vision), horses have a long, thin strip of cells called a visual streak. This gives them a narrow, vertical field of vision. They see very little above and below their eyes when the head is in a neutral position, which is why when they are frightened by something in the distance they will rapidly bob their heads up and down, allowing them a more complete vertical image than if their heads remained still.

Unlike primates, who have hands and therefore need to be able to quickly change their focal distance (such as when you pick up your phone), horses change their focus relatively slowly. They are also slower to adapt to changes of light and dark, which is why good trainers understand the need to give the horse plenty of time to adjust before walking into a darkened trailer or indoor arena. The horse is superbly adapted to see moving objects on the periphery, even in low light, but needs to be 50 per cent closer than a human to see detail. This is because the horse's evolved defence strategies of speed and vigilance do not require detailed visual pictures. The animals that chased and ate horses were at least as large as a wolf, and the horse didn't require great visual acuity to determine the difference between a wolf and, for example, another horse, because firstly they look completely different and secondly the horse has a suite of other exquisitely tuned senses that enable it to determine if something is friend or foe.

Contrary to popular belief, the horse is not colour blind. In nature there is always a trade-off between colour vision and night vision. To put it simply, the mammalian eye has two kinds of light-sensitive cells. Rod cells are responsible for enabling vision in low light and cone cells are responsible for colour vision and high spatial acuity. The ratio of rods to cones in a horse's eye is 20:1, while we have a ratio of 9:1. This means that while we are able to see colours more vividly, the horse will not trip over his own feet in the dark. Colour vision is quite similar in dogs and horses, and while it is impossible to know *exactly* what they see, the best guess is that their colour world is slightly muted, almost as though they were viewing the world through a pale olive-green filter.

The horse has a wonderfully sensitive sense of smell. Obligate nasal breathers, horses can only breathe through their noses, meaning they are smelling more or less constantly. The long face of the horse allows for a large number of olfactory receptors, approximately 300 million. By comparison, humans have 6 million. Horses also outperform us in the number of olfactory genes they possess. We have around 350, horses an impressive 1066, while elephants have the highest number with almost 2000. It's unclear exactly how the number of olfactory genes affects the sense of smell, but it is likely it increases the number of categories of scents that can be detected. In Kenya, elephants can distinguish between the scent of the footprints of the Maasai tribe (who hunt elephants and spear them as a test of manhood) and the footprints of the Kamba tribe (who don't).

Horses smell in stereo. Scents are detected by the nerve-rich mucosa inside the nose and travel directly into the twin olfactory bulbs in the brain. Unlike most of the brain, these structures don't cross over. That is, the left nostril communicates directly with the left olfactory bulb and the right nostril with the right olfactory bulb. This is because olfaction is the oldest of the senses and evolved before bilateral symmetry of the brain. Nerves inside the nose travel directly into the brain, which make it the brain's closest contact with the outside world, because while eyes are basically just bits of extruded brain, the optic nerve is protected by the lens of the eye.

The horse also has an accessory olfactory structure called the vomeronasal organ (VNO). This small depression in the nasal cavity is used to detect pheromones and other volatile odours. Most mammals and some reptiles have VNOs but the existence of a human VNO is still being contested. It appears that, while we have a VNO as embryos, it is less pronounced and visible in adult humans.

In the horse, the VNO has a separate pathway to the brain (the nasopalatine duct) which makes it function as a sensory organ independent of the rest of the horse's olfactory system. Everyone has seen horses 'laugh' or 'smile' by pulling the top lip up and away from the front teeth. This strange posture is called flehmen and is used when the horse is specifically targeting the VNO. This occurs when they smell a particularly unusual smell or when stallions smell mares in oestrus. I have seen my horses perform the flehmen response after being patted by someone who has been smoking, and although it's tempting to think of this as a value judgment about the person's lifestyle choices, it's simply because horses are very rarely exposed to the smell of cigarette smoke and find it worthy of further olfactory exploration.

It seems odd to me that the horse would have evolved two separate systems for smelling. The information from the VNO doesn't travel to the olfactory bulb in the brain via the olfactory nerve; it travels to a different area of the brain. Perhaps it is a different kind of sense, one for which we have no language. Our understanding of the world is so framed by language that it's almost as though things don't exist if we don't have words for them. Maybe one day we will discover that animals have more than five senses but, lacking the words to describe them, we can't conceive of their existence.

The horse's senses of smell and taste are inextricably linked. Not a lot is known about the gustatory sense, but it is assumed it is very sensitive because horses can't vomit, and therefore it's extremely important that they avoid eating toxic plants. Horses have more taste buds than us, coming in at 25,000 compared to our 10,000. They also have similar taste receptors and are motivated to seek out both sweet and salty tastes, and to avoid bitter and sour ones. This is adaptive, because sweet grasses are more calorie-dense and bitter plants are often toxic.

Equine hearing is also much more sensitive than ours. The horse has wonderfully large, mobile ears that can turn through almost 180 degrees. They can hear between 55–33,000 hertz whereas we can only hear between 20–20,000 hertz. I have often wondered about the common practice of leaving a radio playing in stables to calm the occupants. Given their sensitive hearing, it is far more likely to be, at best, annoying and, at worst, painful. Although it would be nice to think horses relax when played classical music, to date, studies have been unable to prove its efficacy. In reality, people have diverse and culturally defined tastes in music and what may be comforting to one person could be grating and discordant to another, so it's quite anthropomorphic to assume horses would have a universal taste in music, or even an appreciation for it.

Horses are tactile creatures and their skin is extremely sensitive. It has been theorized that their entire skin is as sensitive as our fingertips. It's always been fascinating to me to watch a 600-kilogram (94 st) horse shiver a single fly from its skin with remarkable accuracy. Alongside that, the common practice in equestrian sports for riders to wear spurs to make the horse move forwards seems counterintuitive. If the horse's skin is so sensitive, why are spurs so common? I think this is largely because the fundamental mechanisms that drive learning (and therefore habituation) are not always well understood by trainers. I think also that the spectre of tradition looms large in the equestrian world, firmly embedding some practices that might otherwise have died out. But we'll discuss this in much greater detail in the chapters on learning.

Horses are creatures of touch, and they will often stand head to tail and mutually groom each other at the base of the wither. It seems likely that this behaviour strengthens the bonds between individuals in the herd, but it also appears to be relaxing for both participants as studies have shown that it lowers heart rate. Most horses appear to enjoy their human gently scratching the skin at the base of the wither and indeed it is possible to use this as a reward for behaviour. Massage has also been shown to lower heart rate in anxious horses. Andrew McLean has pointed out that much of equestrian practice fails to take into account the horse's desire to be touched. A lot of old school 'breaking in' methods involve keeping the horse at a distance and this does nothing to dispel the horse's inevitable, prey-species anxiety. It's much nicer (for horse and handler) to train with lots of touch.

In the past few decades there has been a shift towards a more horse-centred approach to early training and these methods incorporate the horse's need for touch. I'm very grateful I was exposed to these ways when I was learning about training, because without them I doubt I would ever have become a horse trainer. When I train young horses I always spend several days getting them used to my weight without a saddle. I drape myself over them and gently rub them all over. It's remarkable how their body language changes as they relax, often extending their top lip in the same way they do when they're enjoying a scratch. It's during this period of training that I have often noticed the young horse becomes more curious about people and begins to interact more. I think it's because they learn that humans are a source of comfort and security. This is the part of training I enjoy the most; it's like a cuddle with a purpose and there is undoubtedly some kind of oxytocin release for both of us. I'm not sure who said, 'There's something about the outside of a horse that's good for the inside of a man' but, gender bias aside, they were definitely onto something.

The skin is the horse's largest organ. Just as with humans, the horse's skin is not uniformly innervated — the most sensitive parts of the body are the muzzle, neck, withers, coronet (the small strip of rubbery skin directly above the hoof), shoulders, lower flanks and rear of pastern. I think there's a common misconception that large-hoofed mammals like horses are less sensitive to touch than, for example, lap dogs, but there is no evidence that this is true. The practice of slapping the horse on the neck as a form of reward is problematic as it is so unlike any way that horses interact with each other, and I am certain they enjoy it no more than you or I would. The best way to reward a horse with touch is by scratching at the base of the wither because that's what horses do to each other.

The horse's muzzle is covered with what look like thick hairs. These whiskers are more correctly called vibrissae. There hasn't been a great deal of research on the function of the vibrissae, but it is understood they play an important role in the horse's perceptual abilities. Vibrissae might look like hairs but they're not; they don't moult and they're extremely sensitive. Each vibrissae sits inside a small blood capsule that is rich with nerves, and they can detect the slightest movement. Horses can't see their own mouths so the vibrissae play an important role during grazing — they help determine what is food and what is not. At university we demonstrate to our students how horses discriminate between food and not-food by putting some small wooden blocks and food pellets together in a bucket. Given the gusto with which the university's horses attack the bucket it still amazes me that we've never had a horse eat the wooden blocks. However, the demonstrating horses we use all have a full complement of vibrissae and I definitely wouldn't try the experiment if they didn't.

There's a lot more known about vibrissae in rats, possibly because few people baulk at the ethics of killing large numbers of rodents to study the insides of their brains. In rats the vibrissae are so important that each one connects to an area in the brain dedicated to processing the stimuli. Baby rats, born hairless and blind, nevertheless have vibrissae at birth.

In equestrian sports it has long been common practice to tidy the horse's face by shaving off the vibrissae. Interestingly, I have been told by showjumping riders that this makes the horse less likely to hit fences during competition. I have never seen any studies on that aspect of vibrissae removal, but it suggests that the horse becomes more wary of the environment and more cautious about navigating through it. Until recently it was common practice in some horse sports to also remove the long hairs underneath the horse's eyes which, unsurprisingly, has been shown to increase the incidence of eye injuries. Thankfully the practice has now been banned by the International Federation for Equestrian Sports (FEI) and hopefully other equestrian organizations will follow.

Evaluative richness

While it would be easy to ascribe human emotional states such as jealousy and regret to animals it's very difficult to scientifically validate this. Good science is about testing what we think against what we can prove. It's very easy for us to assume that we think we know how an animal is feeling, but determining it objectively is far harder. While it might be tempting to use our own perspectives to determine emotional states, this is the start of a slippery slope that leads towards anthropocentricism.

Consider this example. Primates are some of our closest non-human relatives, so it would be easy to assume we could instinctively know how they are feeling by their body language and facial gestures. After all, they're just like us, aren't they? When we are surprised or registering disbelief we raise both eyebrows. Yet when capuchin monkeys raise their eyebrows it is an appeasement gesture indicating a lack of aggressive intent. When baboons raise their eyebrows it is a threat gesture. Same taxonomic family, three different species, three totally different uses of the same facial gesture.

At this stage we lack the scientific tools to determine what complex emotions animals are feeling, although no doubt in the future we will develop such tools. For now, the best we can do is ascribe either positive or negative valence to affective states and use the extent and degree to which they occur as a gauge in the measure of consciousness. This might seem like a very blunt instrument with which to measure an animal's undoubtedly rich and complex emotional life, but assuming human emotions can be problematic. After all, if an animal is, for example, hard-working (or possessing of a good work ethic, as many horse people will say) then the reverse can also be true and another animal can be lazy. In a training context this removes the responsibility of the trainer and places the fault at the feet of the horse. Not only is this not useful, it also inadvertently sanctions harsher forms of training because it feels, to the trainer and bystanders, as if they are curing the animal of some kind of character flaw. Thus, much bad training goes unnoticed.

It is far more useful to look at how the horse behaves to determine if something has a positive or negative valence. As we will discuss in far greater detail in Part 2, actions that have reinforcing consequences are more likely to be repeated, whereas actions that have unpleasant consequences are less likely. Remember that sentience is an ability to discriminate between positive and negative perceptual experiences. Training is about responding to either positive or negative perceptual experiences by increasing or decreasing behaviour. Therefore, any animal that can be trained must be considered to possess sentience.

This is interesting because lots of animals most people would not necessarily think of as sentient can be trained. I have seen saltwater crocodiles trained to show their teeth for dental inspections, monitor lizards trained to touch their snouts to a target, and I have read of butterflies being trained to fly to bowls of nectar when cued to do so by a flashing light. All of these animals demonstrate evaluative richness because their behaviour demonstrates that they are clearly able to distinguish and choose between positive and negative affective states.

The number of varying tasks to which the horse has turned its hoof over the past 5000 years is staggering. Not just the expected roles in warfare, agriculture, exploration and sport, but also taking part in pageants and religious ceremonies, as part of mental health therapy, for breed showing, circus, the production of urine for hormone replacement therapy, for producing snake antivenom, for milk . . . it seems that the uses for the horse are almost endless. Yet very rarely do we stop to think if the use we have for the horse is as good for the horse as it is for us. We cannot know if the horse, for example, enjoys racing. Racing journalists and commentators often refer to an individual horse's competitive nature and its desire to win, and they even comment on how proud the horse is after the race. Yet horses do not arrange races amongst themselves. Neither would the winning horse stay in the parade ring after the race to accept the accolades if they were able to leave. Exercise-induced pulmonary haemorrhage, which occurs when the horse's lungs bleed during races, is common in thoroughbreds, and while it is not always useful to make comparisons between humans and other animals, it's hard to imagine running so hard that your lungs bleed.

The same goes for jumping. A large percentage of people involved with jumping horses will tell you that their horse loves jumping. But in my career I have yet to see a horse, when allowed to run loose in a paddock full of jumps, choose to jump them. I cannot imagine that an eventing horse jumping down a drop fence of over 2 metres (6½ ft), and landing on a firm surface carrying a rider of around 80 kilograms (12½ st) does not feel some degree of pain on landing. The uncomfortable truth is that horses rush fences because they are frightened. The flight response, which is the horse's instinct to run from danger, first compels the horse to run away from an object that frightens it, but if that path is not available the horse is still compelled to run. You can't outrun a pack of wolves by standing still. The horse will even run towards things that frighten it because it is the running that gives it some chance of survival.

In my job I often remind myself that I am dealing with a prehistoric brain trying to solve 21st-century problems. In some ways it's a little like kangaroos. If a kangaroo is frightened by an approaching car it will often jump into the road – with disastrous consequences. This is because the kangaroo has not evolved to deal with cars and roads; the kangaroo's flight response and instinct compel it to run (or hop) quickly, but they don't necessarily specify the direction. A zebra's stripes, while primarily to repel flies, also confuse predators because they make it harder to focus on an individual. The kangaroo's erratic flight path works in the same way.

One of the problems of interacting with another species is learning to identify the signals the species uses for varying emotional states and this, as discussed earlier, is difficult even amongst other primates. It was this difficulty which led to the development of what are known as grimace scales — these are objective ways to measure whether an animal is in pain by its facial expressions. Initially developed for laboratory animals (mice, rats and rabbits), the process of developing these scales involves applying painful stimuli to animals, filming their reactions and identifying the facial behaviours common to all of them. The initial work in horses was conducted after routine castrations (done with the horses anaesthetised during the surgery, but given very little pain relief afterwards) but has since been replicated using other kinds of pain including a tourniquet applied to the front leg at 240 mmHg of pressure. (As an aside, in human subjects the upper limit of painful-but-tolerable tourniquet pressure is considered to be about 250 mmHg. In 2017, equitation scientist Orla Doherty conducted a study on 750 competing performance horses and found that nearly 50 per cent of nosebands were so tight that a small plastic wedge known as a taper gauge could not fit between the nasal bone and the noseband. The tightness of these nosebands was estimated to be between 200 and 400 mmHg.)

The equine grimace scale is now a very useful tool for practitioners in all equestrian fields and identifies six main facial expressions common to horses in pain. These include: stiff backwards ears, often with the ears further apart at baseline; eyelids partially or completely closed; contraction of the muscle above the eye; strained chewing muscles above the mouth; more pronounced chin; slightly dilated nostrils. (For interest's sake and as a comparison, the main facial expressions of a mouse in pain include: closing of the eyelid; vertical wrinkles on the side of the nose; bulging of the cheeks; ears becoming more pointed; and whiskers losing their natural downward curve.)

Unity

This realm is all about a single consciousness, a single perspective of the world.

Humans and many animal species process information from the right eye in the left side of the brain and from the left eye in the right side of the brain. The corpus callosum, a thick bundle of nerves that connects the left and right sides of the brain, enables this communication. This ability is called lateralization. Lateralization increases cognitive capacity because each half of the brain becomes a specialist at various tasks and duplication is avoided. It makes it possible for an animal to attend to two separate tasks at once; for example, scanning the environment for predators while also foraging for food. The specialization of brain halves is a great way to eke out the brain's maximum ability, which is necessarily limited by the size of its owner's skull.

There is a remarkable consistency across many animal species in the pattern of lateralization. The left hemisphere directs the animal's attention to specific kinds of stimuli while the right hemisphere processes information relating to novel stimuli (particularly predators), intense emotions and social interactions. This is true of both wild and domesticated species, which indicates that lateralization is not a function of domesticity.

It seems logical to me that the reason we do most of the things we do to horses (lead them, mount them, etc.) is because they prefer to look at scary objects with the left eye first, because the right side of the brain processes information relating to novel stimuli. When I was learning to ride I was told that we mount from the left side because traditionally soldiers wore swords on the left side of the body (so they could draw them with their right hand) and it made mounting easier. But it's far more likely that, over time, how we interact with horses has developed to best manage the ways in which they perceive the world.

An interesting side effect of lateralization is the ability of some species to perform unihemispheric sleep; that is, one side of the brain sleeps while the other is awake. Dolphins, seals and manatees can all sleep with one side of the brain at a time, allowing them to rest while also remaining vigilant to predators. Many bird species also use unihemispheric sleep, particularly while on long migratory flights.

Like us, the horse doesn't sleep with one side of the brain at once. However, it can sleep while standing up, thanks to a unique stay apparatus in the legs. This arrangement of muscles, tendons and ligaments stabilizes the legs and enables most types of sleep. It is only during REM (rapid eye movement) sleep that the horse has to lie down, because during REM sleep changes occur in brain signalling, and this causes what's known as muscle atonia or reduced muscle function. Horses don't need as much REM sleep as humans; they can get by on between 40 and 60 minutes while most adult humans should have at least 90 minutes every 24 hours. The horse's total overall requirements for sleep are lower than ours, too: they need between three and five hours sleep every 24 hours, whereas for optimal health adult humans should get between seven and eight hours. Unsurprisingly, recent research has shown that horses that cannot see other horses while lying down (as would be the case in most modern stables) have less REM sleep than horses that have close visual contact with their peers. In humans, a lack of REM sleep has significant implications on memory formation and we can only assume that the same effects would occur in horses.

Unlike humans, horses are not diurnal. That is, they are not active all day and sleepy at night; rather, their sleep occurs throughout a 24-hour period in short bursts. They get most of their REM sleep in the very early hours of the morning, before dawn. This is most likely because many predators are crepuscular, meaning they are most active at dawn and dusk.

Temporality

This realm is all about the ability to mentally time travel; that is, to remember the past at will and imagine the future. This is a complex and highly specialized skill. So far the best evidence of it in the animal kingdom is in great apes (orangutans, gorillas, chimpanzees), cetaceans (whales, dolphins), corvids (crows, ravens) and cephalopods (octopuses).

Interestingly, this seems like an ability that would benefit animals with a hard-to-find (or hard-to-catch) food source. Which isn't the horse — as American writer Stephen Budiansky points out, grass, unlike mice, cannot hide. Species that have seasonally available food sources, such as the orcas that hunt migrating chinook salmon, or species that cache food such as woodpeckers and rooks, are those that would benefit most from developing the ability to mentally project an image of themselves into the past and future.

Temporality is also related to the ability to understand that objects exist even when they are out of sight. This is called object permanence and was first documented in the 1950s by psychologist Jean Piaget. Most of us have played the 'peekaboo' game with a baby or very young toddler. The rules are simple: you cover your face with your hands and remove them quickly (usually also saying 'boo' or 'peekaboo'). This game is hugely enjoyable for the child because their brains are developing an understanding of an important rule, namely that even if an object (that's you) cannot be seen or sensed it still continues to exist.

In the past couple of decades, research into object permanence in animals has become increasingly widespread as it provides insight into the ways in which animals perceive their world. To me, it is a little similar to the research into language acquisition, though the process of determining an animal's object permanence abilities is far less arduous. I think it's important to avoid assessing an animal's ability and grading this relative to ours. The ability to understand that out-of-sight objects continue to exist has undoubtedly evolved to fulfil some purpose in an animal's life cycle, just as it evolved to fulfil a purpose in our ancestors'. The degree to which an animal demonstrates object permanence is not an indicator of intelligence (because that's an anthropocentrically loaded concept) — it's simply a reflection of the pressures placed upon it by evolution.

The process of assessing object permanence usually involves getting an animal to retrieve a hidden food treat. This is done by placing food in one of three containers while the animal watches, momentarily concealing those containers behind screens and then revealing them and allowing the animal to choose where the food is. Generally, each container has a small sample of food taped into it to avoid the animal being able to smell their way to the correct answer. Instead, they must rely on knowing which container they saw the food placed into. It's an interesting exercise but very biased towards species that have complex food sources or that store food, for which this kind of cognitive ability would be a necessity. These tests usually require an ability to focus intently in a way that might actually be quite maladaptive in a species like the horse, which is always vigilant for the approach of predators.

Despite my misgivings, though, I think research into object permanence can give some valuable insights into ways in which animals perceive their world, and those insights can inform the choices we make about housing, training and transport.

For instance, if a social animal like the horse has limited object permanence it would be extremely stressful to isolate him from members of the herd, even if only for short periods, because he cannot reason that his herd will be there when he returns. Horses are often stabled and transported in isolation. Studies have shown that providing them with mirrors, while not as effective as providing other horses, can reduce their stress levels, but even better would be a world in which we cannot perceive the necessity of isolating them in the first place.

Object permanence is not a yes/no ability, it's a sliding scale in which an animal's ability to reason the continuing existence of an object gets increasingly more complex.

Taking the stress out of training

Understanding how the brain of the horse works is, for me, a good way to make training as stress-free as possible. As part of my job, I sometimes travel to other properties or farms to help people train their horses. Daisy and Simon are two thoroughbreds that live together happily and I enjoy training them because their conscientious owner tries very hard to keep them in a way that is not at odds with their evolution. They rarely wear rugs, they don't get stabled or isolated from each other and their diet is mostly roughage. However, the one thing she can't provide them with is a herd. I often find that horses in these situations get very bonded to each other and Daisy and Simon are no exception — they are like a happily married couple.

The paddock next to the arena contains a large open shed and we discovered that if Simon was being trained and Daisy had grazed her way behind the shed (so that she couldn't be seen) Simon started to get anxious. It's always best to avoid anxiety during training, not just for welfare reasons but also because there is a risk that the training scenario itself will become a cue for anxiety, which is problematic. We needed a way of training Simon without anxiety, but one that would gradually make him resilient to Daisy's absence. So we began by giving Daisy some extra hay where Simon could see her and gradually, week by week, we moved the hay a little further away from the arena. Now, after several months, Simon stays calm even when Daisy goes out of sight, though if she finds a particularly tasty patch of grass behind the shed and is out of sight for longer than a few minutes, he starts to look intently at the place where she disappeared. I don't think for a moment that we have trained Simon to somehow achieve object permanence but, by understanding the fundamental structures underlying his behaviour, we've been able to work around it.

Self-awareness

Self-awareness is the conscious awareness of yourself as separate from the world outside. The recognition of self, or selfhood, is not binary but rather exists on a continuum. Where an animal sits on that continuum is not necessarily a reflection of their cognitive ability, but reflects the pressures exerted upon the brain during evolution. Or to put it more simply: if you don't need it, you don't have it.

You can think of each organism on the planet as being like the latest model of a particular motor vehicle: they all have features specific to their purpose. There are four-wheel drives, sports cars, family wagons and motorbikes. Not one of them has all the features because it would be difficult, for example, to build a sports car that could go from 0 to 100 in 6 seconds, could drive comfortably up a sand dune while carrying seven passengers plus a load of shopping, and which only has two wheels. Features are expensive and, to a certain extent, self-limiting. Vehicles will come only with the features their purchaser is likely to use. The same is true of evolution. Organisms only come equipped with the traits they need to survive in their specific environmental niche, and possibly a handful of vestigial traits that were once useful but which they no longer need.

Self-awareness is a complex and therefore expensive evolutionary trait, and it exists in its most developed form in just a few animal species. These include dolphins, orcas, chimps, bonobos, orangutans, gorillas, magpies, Asian elephants (controversially) and (even more controversially) cleaner wrasse fish.

The test for self-awareness was developed in 1970 by a psychologist called Gordon Gallup. In this test, first performed on chimps, an animal is given access to a mirror and its reactions are very carefully gauged. Eventually, a researcher paints the animal with two small, odourless dye spots. One is placed where the animal can see it in the mirror and the other (which is the control) is placed in a hard-to-see spot. An animal is said to pass the mirror test if it investigates the visible dye spot in the mirror but ignores the control.

In the first experiment Gallup's chimps were marked with a dye spot on their brows. When they saw themselves in the mirror they used the mirror to rub the dye off — they didn't try to rub the dye from the chimp in the mirror. Subsequent versions of the test have all revealed interesting facets of an animal's cognition. For example, elephants did not pass when the mirror was small and out of reach but when the researchers presented them with a large, elephant-proof mirror they used it to look inside their own mouths and to explore the dye spots on their heads. They even placed food in front of the mirror and then watched themselves eat it.

Horses do not pass the mirror test and neither do dogs or human infants younger than about eighteen months old. Babies don't pass because the human brain takes a long time to develop. It's possible that horses and dogs don't pass because their primary sense is not vision but smell. The mirror doesn't smell like a horse (or a dog) and therefore lacks the essential markers for 'horseness'. On our training arena at home we have mirrors so that riders can see themselves in the saddle. When horses are first shown the mirrors most of them are quite startled. Up close the thing in the mirror looks like a horse but it lacks the other features that make it a horse, such as smell, various pheromones, body heat, sounds, etc. Many horses attempt to touch noses with the horse in the mirror and some (particularly stallions) will squeal and even strike out with a front leg, but after a couple of minutes they almost all usually lose interest.

Galloping Galileo

I had a friend who owned a rather lovely stallion called Galileo. One spring, when he was young, full of hormones and the intent to use them, Galileo's owner decided to allow him to roam around her property so he could eat some long grass and save her the job of trimming it. It was a beautiful sunny day, and he was peacefully grazing so she went inside to get herself some lunch. She was just sitting down with her sandwich when she heard banging and squealing. She rushed outside to discover that Galileo was staging a full-blown battle with the reflection of himself that he could see on the side of her brand-new, super-shiny (and expensive) horse float. Luckily, Galileo survived the battle unscathed, though the horse float was never quite the same again.

Like object permanence and language acquisition, self-recognition is not a test of intelligence; it's a unique adaptation to a specific set of environmental challenges. Just because humans do it doesn't mean it is the pinnacle of cognitive achievement. It's just one of a countless number of mental abilities that animals possess, the vast majority of which we still know nothing about. The small amount of information we have now about these abilities offers us a tiny window with which to look into the minds of animals, but this in no way gives us a complete picture. It's perhaps ironic that our own specific language acquisition skill — the skill that enabled us to take dominion over the natural world, and the skill that frames our perception and understanding of reality — may indeed limit our understanding of the world only to things that we can describe.

~

This concludes the history, ethology and cognition section of the book. From here on we'll adopt a more hands-on approach and look at ways that the horse learns. These ways are common to all animal species and humans too (though this is somewhat complicated by our big, prefrontal cortex). While it's tempting to jump straight into the training, I think it's important to truly understand the horse before beginning.

It's difficult not to feel a sense of awe when you truly know the horse. He is not our partner, our friend or our slave. He is not a pet, a therapist or a tool for the human ego, but a masterpiece of evolution, perfectly adapted for ancient life on the plains but (with sensitive, considered training and management) perfectly able to thrive in the 21st century.

PART 2:

WAYS OF LEARNING

A few years ago I got a call from a man called Max who said that he would like some help training camels.

'Sure,' I said. 'But I haven't had a great deal of experience training camels.'

'That's all right, neither have I,' he said and then went on to explain that the camels were feral and had just recently been caught.

'Great,' I said. 'Though I haven't had a great deal of experience training feral animals.'

'That's okay, neither have I,' he said, then told me he was planning to start a dairy.

'Great,' I said. 'Though I haven't had a lot of experience training dairy animals.'

He said, 'That's okay, neither have I.'

We decided that the best course of action would be for him to get the camels used to his presence and attempt to teach them to eat out of a bucket, at first placed on the ground but eventually while it was being held. With a great deal more confidence than I felt, I said that I was keen to get started and would see him in a couple of weeks.

Just as we were finalizing our plans he said, 'Oh and by the way I'm blind and I have a guide dog. Do you think that will be a problem?'

'Not in comparison to the rest,' I said.

A few weeks later we drove to meet Max at his farm. He met us at the gate and by his side was the most beautiful labrador guide dog I've ever seen. As glossy as an otter, Forest was 40 or so kilograms of intelligence and barely contained joy. I liked Max from the moment we first met, not just because he was saving animals that would otherwise be culled but also because he forgave me for failing to read the 'Please don't touch me. I'm working' writing on Forest's harness and having a love-at-first-sight wrestle on the ground at his feet with his dog.

When I had extricated my arm from Forest's mouth and wiped off some of the saliva, we wandered over to the yards where the camels were waiting. I don't think I'd ever been close to a camel before, and my first impression was that they were

BIG. Much taller than a horse, camels are cow-smelling and soft-footed. Horse's legs are refined, the tendons like wire beneath the skin and the joints hard. Camels and cows always look to me as though they have swollen legs, the tendons are barely visible and the legs almost slump to the fetlock. Once you stop comparing, though, they're beautiful, with huge, slow-blinking eyes thickly fringed with dark lashes. They move with a loose-hipped fluidity that's quiet across the ground and surprisingly fast. They're also perfectly adapted for life in the desert. They store fat in their humps and they can close their nostrils to avoid inhaling sand in a storm. Sadly, their ability to thrive in the Australian desert has meant that they are now considered pests and are often culled.

Max's camels regarded us with quiet curiosity from behind their movie star lashes. Although many stations cull camels by shooting them from helicopters, sometimes they will muster and sell them instead. The twelve female camels in the yard didn't realize it, but if it hadn't been for Max they wouldn't have been alive. He had also done a great job getting them used to the presence of humans and to the idea of camel cubes, tasty (if you're a camel) high-calorie pellets which to animals that have spent a lifetime foraging in the desert must seem like a bucketful of free chocolate cake.

~

The first behaviour that is often taught to untrained animals is to touch their nose (or beak or foot) to a target. You can buy custom-made targets but I use a worn-out tennis ball with a small cut in it, wedged onto an old riding crop. Targeting is a simple behaviour, surprisingly quick to train and a good way to offer any animal an insight into the rules of a great new game. When the animal touches the target with their nose, the trainer makes a distinctive noise and then offers a tasty treat as a reward. Pretty soon the animal learns that the distinctive noise precedes and therefore predicts the treat, and the noise becomes a marker for the correct behaviour. This relatively simple behaviour utilizes both operant conditioning (positive reinforcement) and classical conditioning (the connection between the noise and the food).

The distinctive noise becomes what is known as a conditioned reinforcer and it's a far more efficient way of training than trying to deliver the reward directly to the animal's mouth exactly as the behaviour you want to reinforce is occurring. The noise simply tells the animal that the reward is on its way. It's not a cue for behaviour and it is never given without a reward. Think of it as simply affirming that the learner has given the correct response, like saying 'Yes!'

Of course, you must pair the conditioned reinforcer with something that the animal desires. Food, stroking, play, sex and freedom are reinforcing (to human and non-human animals, let's be honest), but in a training context food and stroking are the most commonly used. When initial training is done with wild animals, food is the most commonly used reinforcer, though I have seen videos of aquariums where stingrays have been trained for belly rubs.

One of the most commonly used conditioned reinforcers is a small device that when pressed makes a very distinctive click sound. Unsurprisingly, it's called a clicker. When I was first starting out training this way I used a party favour plastic cricket and it worked perfectly. Now, because of the widespread use of clickers amongst dog trainers you can buy ergonomic clickers in a huge variety of colours and shapes, but I must admit I sometimes remember my party favour clicker with fondness. Back then, training in this way felt almost like an act of defiance — people viewed it as bribery and thought it would make animals greedy or lead to biting. Of course, that has been proven not to be the case, and indeed, when you see an agility dog working with what looks like absolute joy, you can be pretty certain it has been trained by someone skilled in the use of conditioned reinforcers.

The reason animal trainers often use a clicker is because the sound is both salient and consistent; these two factors are required for a strong connection between the two classically conditioned elements. Throughout my career I've experimented with lots of different conditioned reinforcers. A single word can work well, but a lot of animals are quite habituated to the sound of the human voice so it's not always salient and, because of human error, not always consistent. When we train elephants in Thailand the mahouts usually gather around to watch. It's not uncommon for everyone to get involved in the training process and when the elephant performs the correct behaviour there will be a chorus of, 'Good. Very good. Good, good, very good . . .' from the viewers. I suppose I resist the use of words as conditioned reinforcers because often trainers forget that their learner recognizes the sound of the word and not its meaning. And to me it's still a bit too anthropocentric. Language is human. I like to meet an animal on a level playing field, stripped bare of the quirk that has given my species the belief that the world is ours.

Whistles are also useful as conditioned reinforcers. When you're training, there is no such thing as a behaviour vacuum: the learner is never between behaviours. So if you're too slow to reinforce the behaviour you want, you usually end up reinforcing the one that followed, or the one after that. Which means that whatever you use as a conditioned reinforcer must be able to be used immediately. Therefore, if you choose a whistle, it's got to be kept in your mouth throughout the training session — and finding one that's comfortable can be difficult. A high-frequency dog whistle works but it's hard to tell if you're using it consistently (in terms of the length of the sound) because it's only barely audible to human ears. Also, try holding something in your mouth that's the diameter of a pencil and you'll soon notice that you dribble quite a lot — though you can get around this by shoving the end of the whistle into a short piece of surgical tube that can be pinched a little more easily between your teeth.

Whistles are widely used as conditioned reinforcers by marine mammal trainers. If you look at videos from aquariums you'll see that the trainers almost always have a whistle between their teeth. I assume the whistle has been chosen for its ability to be heard underwater and also because anything held in the hand would quickly become covered with fish insides and scales. I love looking at live fish, but I can't stand the smell of dead ones and I'm not sure I could ever habituate to that smell. Luckily for me, horses are herbivorous.

I decided to use a clicker as a conditioned reinforcer with the camels because I'm more practiced with its use and therefore less likely (though, sadly, still quite likely) to make mistakes. So, when we climbed into the yards, we took a clicker, a bucket of camel pellets and the target. We moved slowly and the camels were interested and calm. Max had predicted that the largest female, a gorgeous light-coloured lady who would tower over any horse I've ever worked with, would be the first to approach us and he was right. Outside, we'd rubbed the target in the bucket of pellets, hoping that the smell would entice one of the camels to investigate. Now, when Max held the target towards her she dropped her head to investigate and I clicked then held the bucket out so she could take a mouthful. After about ten repetitions of this she learned that humans could become vending machines of tasty treats if she put in the very minimal effort of touching her nose to the target.

Pretty soon Max could walk away from the camel and when he held out the target she would walk up to him so she could touch her nose to the target. I followed half a step behind with the bucket. It was calm, almost peaceful, and when she'd had enough she simply turned and walked back to the rest of her small herd. I remember driving home later that afternoon, playing the session over in my head and smiling.

As a trainer it's my job to make sure the training process is not stressful to the animal and that they leave the session feeling comfortable and content. Sometimes living alongside humans can be very confusing. Why is it okay to lie on this mat but not on the double bed? Or to buck in the paddock but not under saddle? Scratch this post but not the lounge? Chew this toy but not this shoe? Many people's pets arrive at the correct behaviour via a circuitous route of many, many errors. And maybe domestic animals have been inadvertently selectively bred for their ability to cope with stress. I find conflict of every type aversive so, like most animal trainers, I try to work error-free. That is, we try to curate the learning process so that the animal always knows the answer to the question before we ask it.

Error-free learning was first documented by professor of psychology Herbert Terrace, who was trying to train pigeons to discriminate between a horizontal and a vertical line. Pigeons that learned this task by trial and error usually made over 1000 errors before they achieved it and they often remained agitated and slow to respond even once the behaviour was well established. Terrace changed the way the task was trained. First, he taught his pigeons to peck a green light and not a red one, then he superimposed a horizontal line over the green light and a vertical one over the red. Slowly he faded out the light and by the time it was gone completely the pigeons were reliably choosing the horizontal light every time. Interestingly, I've seen police dogs trained in a similar way. First, they are taught to seek out their favourite toy, then a small quantity of drugs or explosives is taped to the toy and they are taught to seek that out. Remove the toy and the dog will find the drugs, assuming of course that the toy is given as a reward the instant they do.

Watching animal training should be about as entertaining as watching a kindergarten class learn to chant the alphabet. Learning requires neurons in the brain to change and develop and that, just like training the rest of the body, takes time. That's why I don't like televised training; it's too tempting to try to make a methodical, systematic process entertaining. In the few televised training shows that I have seen I was amazed how far people had allowed the relationship between themselves and their animal to deteriorate, but I suppose that, for many people, asking for help is an admission that they have failed in some way. Regret and recrimination are just self-administered punishment and, like every good animal trainer, I'm very wary of punishment.

Max has since become a wonderful, ethical trainer. He has a scientist's brain, so he uses traditional camel-training methods tempered by his knowledge of operant and classical conditioning. He has designed an in-the-field milking machine so the camels don't have to leave their pasture to be milked, and everything he does with his camels is centred around maximizing their wellbeing. His operation has grown, and once this year's calves have been born, he will have over 40 camels to milk every day.

One of the many, many gifts animal training has bestowed upon me over the years is the people I've met who are prepared to do everything they can to keep their animals happy. It's absolutely beautiful to see a 3-metre (10-ft) saltwater crocodile blissfully position his face under a cold hose, or a rehabilitated peregrine falcon stoop with unbelievable speed to a lure, or a young horse take its first wobbly steps under saddle or a feral camel quietly step up to a target. But for me a big part of the joy of those experiences is getting to know the person behind the animal. A person who has undoubtedly given up no small portion of their life to studying, raising and keeping their animal. And who will do whatever it takes to curate for their animal, not just a life, but a life worth living.

~

When I was a kid, a common debate was whether, if given one wish, it would be cooler to fly, to become invisible or to communicate with animals. To me there was no decision to be made: it was animals every time. And I sometimes wonder if this wish is what my entire career has been built around. Because in the moment when you first train an animal and the connection is created, you suddenly have a way of communicating. It doesn't matter if the learner is a thoroughbred racehorse, a battery hen or a feral camel — in that moment it feels like something magical has happened. Some animal trainers call it the 'aha moment,' but it's more than that because training is not something you do *to* an animal, it's something you do *with* an animal. That moment opens a window between two species; it is always memorable and, to me, always profound.

In the late-nineteenth century a Polish ophthalmologist, L.L. Zamenhof, created Esperanto, a language he hoped would become the universal second language of choice for countries all over the world. A language with which to unite the world. The ways in which we all learn are an inter-species Esperanto, the hardwiring for which we are all born with. It's a form of communication common to us all. When you approach an animal with a thorough understanding of the ways in which learning occurs, you are not expecting it to venture into the human realm of language, nor are you trying to blunder your way into the animal's own form of communication. Rather, you are meeting on ground that is common to both of you because the fundamental mechanisms work the same, regardless of species.

On a long flight home from a training clinic, I met a young man who worked in the far north of Western Australia. He told me that every few months he would drive to the most remote place he could and camp for a few days because, as he said, 'I need to feel that I'm unimportant and small compared to the world around me.' And I understand what he means. We all need to feel awe. To be amazed and humbled by the world we live in. To see it with new eyes. For me, that moment occurs when I meet an animal on common ground. We are no more and no less than each other. We are two beings that have slipped through the cracks of this world to a place where we are not divided by our differences but united by what we share.

SARAH

2018

Sarah strokes the neck of the old brown horse.

'Good boy, Jack,' she says as she gently combs her fingers through his mane. In her pocket she has a bag of liquorice and he nudges her hip, his long top lip rustling the plastic packet through the fabric of her jeans.

'I brought raspberry,' she smiles, 'because I know it's your favourite.' She offers him some on her palm. She watches him eat, the deep shadowed hollows above his eyes and his soft muzzle roaned with grey.

He chews slowly, eyes half-closed and glassy with the sweetness. She rests her forehead against his cheek and breathes in the smell of him. It was the smell she fell in love with first – warm sunlight, shining flanks and crushed grass. When she was young that was the smell of the paddocked horses she fed with stalks of plucked grass on a family holiday, and of dusty-coated fairground ponies, but later as she got older it became, for her, the smell of happiness.

~

'Horse mad,' her mother would say as she watched her young daughter canter and neigh on the grassy verge of their shady suburban neighbourhood. 'She'll grow out of it.'

She said it again years later, when Sarah lined the walls of her bedroom with posters of horses and filled her bookshelf with books about horses. 'She'll grow out of it.'

And when she saved all her birthday presents and pocket money for riding lessons: 'She'll grow out of it.'

But she didn't. By the time she was thirteen Sarah was working at the local riding school every weekend in return for rides. And every Sunday afternoon, dirt smeared and exhausted, she would come home and cram her homework, sometimes falling asleep at her desk with her head on the books.

'Maybe not horse mad,' she once heard her mother say as she gently shook her awake. 'Just plain mad.'

Every second weekend she stayed at her dad's house but his new wife was allergic to horses and didn't like the dirty boots by the front door of their apartment. Sarah always knew when they were arguing about her because when she walked into the room they would stop talking, Dad would look empty somehow and Alexandra would press her lips together in a hard line.

One day, while they were driving to the stables, Dad told her it would be easier if she stopped staying over for a while. 'You and I will still see each other and I'll come and watch you ride,' he said. 'It will only be for a little while.' Sarah, who tried to blink away the stinging in her eyes, watched his hands on the steering wheel and nodded. 'That's a good girl,' he said briskly. 'I knew you'd understand.'

That was the day she first saw Jack. He arrived at the riding school on a trailer that seemed more rust than metal, and she heard him kicking the sides as it rattled down the long limestone driveway. The man who dropped the tailgate had a cigarette on his bottom lip and he threw the rope at her, shrugged and said, 'Good luck.'

She led the horse to the yards, all hips and ribs and his mane straggling to his shoulder. He snorted, a new moon of white in his eye and his feet so splayed and cracked she was sure he would trip over them.

When Jane, the owner of the riding school, arrived later that day she took one look at the new horse in the yards and shook her head.

'Oh hell,' she said. 'I'd send him back but nobody else wants him. It's gonna to take months before he looks decent and his feet are just bloody awful.'

Sarah, who was carefully brushing the tangles from his long mane, looked up and said, 'I think he's beautiful.'

'Well, don't get too attached to him, love. He started life as a racehorse and failed at that. Then he tried polo, failed at that. Last I heard he'd failed as a showjumper, too. This is the end of the line. If he fails at being a riding school horse it's off to the doggers, I'm afraid.' And she sawed her fingertips across her neck for emphasis.

Sarah nodded but as soon as Jane walked away she whispered into the horse's neck, 'People are just awful, sometimes. Don't worry, I know you're going to be great.'

But as the weeks and months went by it became apparent that he wasn't great. He was hard to catch. He pulled away when he was tied up and broke ropes, kicked out at the farrier, bit when the girth was being tightened and, one rainy day, when the wind blew a chaff bag past the arena, he spun and bucked so hard that Jane fell off. Sarah thought he should have been forgiven for bucking but Jane's new boyfriend, Dave, was watching and Jane fell off next to the gate, where the horses' feet churned the puddles to mud. It didn't help that Dave laughed so hard he dropped his beer or that Jane was wearing brand new jodhpurs.

'That's it!' yelled Jane. 'This bloody animal has had enough chances. I'm calling the knackers on Monday.'

Sarah, who had caught Jack and was leading him back to the yards, suddenly turned cold beneath her jacket. She imagined Jack, now glossy-coated and sleek, herded into a yard along with all the other horses no one wanted — the ponies too old to be ridden, slow racehorses and jumpers with damaged tendons. She shivered and thought about how frightened he'd be, and though she blinked as hard as she could, she couldn't stop the tears from sliding out.

Eventually, when Jane had changed into dry jodhpurs, she came and found Sarah in Jack's yard. 'I can't keep him, you know that don't you?'

Sarah wiped her nose on her sleeve.

'I mean, I know you like him but he's no good to me. I've got a business to run.'

Sarah nodded slowly, her face damp.

'That's a good girl,' said Jane briskly. 'I knew you'd understand.'

As Sarah rode her bike home that afternoon, she decided she was tired of trying to understand adults. It seemed to her that they did what was easy, even if it wasn't right. Horses were never born naughty, they just learned to be that way because sometimes people were awful. And it didn't seem fair to her that Jack was going to die for something that wasn't his fault. She decided she would take him away and hide him until she could come up with a plan to save his life.

That night when her mother was at her Pilates class, Sarah filled her school backpack with muesli bars, a raincoat and a sleeping bag. She left her jodhpurs and jumper beneath her pyjamas, and when her mother got home, Sarah pretended to be asleep, with the covers pulled up past her ears. She was tired and it was hard to stay awake, but just after midnight she got out of bed and quietly let herself out of the house. She muffled the sound of the gate latch with her hand, wheeled her bicycle down the driveway and out onto the road.

There was no moon that night and the tree shadows were bleak and skeletal. She told herself the darkness would keep her from being discovered but her heartbeat was making it hard to breathe and her mouth was dry.

By the time she got to the stables it was 1.30 in the morning. She let herself into the tack room, hid her bike under a pile of rugs and stuffed a long rope and a bridle into her backpack. Then she walked into Jack's yard and quietly whispered to him, 'It's just me, Jack. We have to get you out of here.' He sniffed her outstretched hands and let her buckle on his headcollar. His hooves sounded too loud on the gravel driveway, and when he skittered a little at the letterbox, Sarah drew a deep breath waiting for lights to turn on in the house. But it remained dark.

Down the road they went in the shadows of the trees. The night was dense and Sarah soon realized that Jack could see better than she could, so she let him pick his own way along the verge. They turned off the road and onto a sandy track, and though it seemed even darker in the bush, Jack walked beside her calmly with his ears pricked, and for a moment Sarah allowed herself a small smile. In the nearby national park was a hiking trail that ran for hundreds of kilometres, all the way to the sea — and there were huts and, more importantly, water tanks. Sarah wasn't sure what she would eat but she knew that they could drink and that there would be grass for Jack along the way.

They came to the first hut as the sun was rising above the hills to the east. By tying the long rope from tree to tree, Sarah made a yard for Jack and while he pulled up mouthfuls of winter grass she sat in the doorway of the hut and ate a muesli bar. Magpies sang in the trees above and the first bees began to forage in the weeds along the path. She leaned her head against the door frame and closed her eyes.

She wasn't sure what woke her, but when she opened her eyes the sun was well over the hills. 'Come on then, Jack,' she said. 'We've got a long way to go.'

As the day went on it became obvious to Sarah that riding boots were not meant for walking. Her feet ached and by lunchtime there were angry blisters on each heel. Still, she knew that she couldn't stop walking. When they made it to the second hut that afternoon she took off her boots and socks. Her feet were a mess, with blisters on her heels and raw patches between her toes. That night she slept in the doorway of the hut so she could see Jack and hear him. It was cold in her sleeping bag and she curled into a ball, her stomach empty and protesting about the single muesli bar that she'd eaten for dinner.

The next morning there was frost on the ground and it looked like the edges of things were painted silver, like a Christmas card. She tried to cover the weeping blisters on her feet with muesli bar wrappers before she put on her socks but she couldn't get them to stay in place. She stopped trying after a while and, wincing, pulled on her boots.

By mid-afternoon Sarah's feet were so sore she could only hobble. She was dizzy with tiredness and was running out of muesli bars. She sat down on a tree stump and felt the tears close at the backs of her eyes. She suddenly realized that even if she wanted to give up she had no idea where she was or how to get home. She put her head in her hands and began to sob.

A moment later she felt the nudge of a soft muzzle against her arm. She stroked Jack's face with her fingertips. 'How am I going to save you when I'm so hopeless I can't even walk?' He nudged her again and lowered his head so she could scratch his ears. She straightened his forelock and blew her nose on her sleeve. She looked down at her feet and, beside them, Jack's hooves. 'At least you can still walk,' she said and paused, thinking. 'Maybe you can walk for the both of us?'

She pulled the bridle from her bag and gently slipped it over his ears, smoothing the soft skin of his head beneath the leather. Then she pulled him a little closer and leaned over him, talking and stroking his neck. He didn't move when she slithered onto his back, and she sat quietly for a moment before brushing his sides with her heels. 'Let's go,' she breathed. And as he swung into an easy walk she smiled and gently scratched his wither.

She would never forget that first ride, the bush scrolling slowly past and the late afternoon light slanting through the trees. Her feet throbbed and her head was all cottony with hunger, but she couldn't ever remember feeling so free. And that night, though her whole body ached for food and a warm bed, as she lay in her sleeping bag watching Jack crop the grass she knew that she was doing the right thing.

The next day her feet were so sore that she could hardly walk, she was dizzy and she felt sick. She used a fallen log to get onto Jack and he walked, she thought, as though he knew he had to look after her. She swayed on his back, closing her eyes against the bright winter sun, half asleep on his back with her fingers wound through his mane.

She never remembered arriving at the next hut, but the hikers who found her there said that even half-conscious she wouldn't let go of the reins unless they promised not to let anything happen to Jack. When she woke up she was in hospital and her mother was in a chair by the bed.

'Sarah, thank god you're okay,' she said, and her eyes were red from crying. 'We thought we'd never find you. I love you but, also you're grounded till you're at least twenty. Maybe 25.'

'Jack?'

'He's fine, in much better shape than you are.'

Sarah began to cry with her face in her hands. 'I have to get out of here. I can't let them take him away.'

'They won't, Sarah. They can't. He's yours now.'

It wasn't always easy after that. There were times when she sat in the dust of the arena, crying while Jack galloped around with his head in the air. But she believed in the little brown horse that no one else wanted, and slowly he began to improve. They went to pony club together, then competitions, and eventually the walls of her bedroom were covered with rosettes they had won.

She cried into his neck when the girls at school were awful to her and when John Macarthur broke her heart. Jack was the first to hear about her engagement and he was the first horse her daughters ever rode. But at twenty, arthritis swelled Jack's joints and by 25 each step he took was slow and painful.

~

Sarah pulls the last piece of raspberry liquorice from her pocket and Jack shuffles closer, his old legs knobbled with age. Though he stands fetlock-deep in lush grass, Sarah can see the shadow of his ribs and the hollows in front of his hip bones. Though her cheeks are wet with tears she rests her forehead against his cheek.

'Thank you,' she says. 'For everything.'

She watches him take the very last piece of liquorice from her palm then turns to where the vet is standing, just outside the gate, and nods.

6.

OPERANT CONDITIONING

Many different species of animals live alongside us. Some, like birds and rodents, are wild and their interactions with us are mostly just avoidant. Some, like horses, dogs and other domesticated species, are forced to interact with us on a daily basis. For their own wellbeing and ours, it's important that these interactions are calm and predictable. The best way to achieve this is, of course, through effective training.

Even animals that have been domesticated for thousands of years aren't born knowing the rules of human interactions. They may have been selected for slightly reduced instincts compared to their wild counterparts, but the instincts are still there. It's really easy to see this when we compare the prey drive of domestic dogs to other cooperatively hunting canines such as wolves. In wolves, the prey drive has five component parts: searching, stalking, chasing, biting to grab and biting to kill. Most domestic dogs show just a part of this drive, and few show the biting to kill component unless they have been specifically bred for it. Selective breeding of working dogs hijacks one part of the prey drive sequence so, for example, pointers demonstrate the search and stalk components, border collies the stalk and chase, while many of the terrier breeds show the chase and bite parts of the sequence. Managing some of these breeds in a domestic environment requires careful training and management — it's very sad to see a magnificent working dog, bred to stalk and chase livestock, locked in a small suburban backyard with nothing to do, and hardly surprising when they become adept at escaping, then stalking and chasing down the mailman.

Managing the prey drive in domestic dogs is a lot like managing the flight response in domestic horses. It requires careful training. As we have already discussed, horse riding is statistically one of the most dangerous sports you can participate in and much of the risk stems from miscommunication between horse and rider. However, it has been shown that when an evidence-based training strategy is utilized the risk significantly decreases. The flight response has served wild horses well for millennia but it is very often a factor when riders are injured. Horses will run away, not only from things that frighten them but also from things they do not understand. This includes bad or unclear training. When dangerous behaviours such as bucking, rearing, swerving, shying and bolting are all parts of the flight response, it's easy to see why good training is so important.

Rugging

So much of what we do with horses we do because of inadvertent anthropomorphism. Stabling and rugging are two that seem particularly rooted in our own feelings. We like the idea that the horse gets tucked into her stable at night in the same way that we tuck ourselves into bed. But, as we discussed previously, horses are not diurnal, so a stable is less a bed and more a place of confinement.

Rugging is also a behaviour that stems largely from our need to nurture the horse in the same way that we would nurture another human. We need warm jackets when the weather gets cool because humans have a thermoneutral zone between 25° and 30°C (77–86°F) (essentially, the temperature at which we are comfortable without clothes) but the horse has a very different thermoneutral zone between 5° and 25°C (41–77°F).

This means that the horse really does not need a rug on a crisp day when we would need a jacket to be comfortable.

Most of the rest of this book is dedicated to a discussion of evidence-based training modalities, which include operant conditioning, classical conditioning and habituation. These are scientific sounding words for processes that are, in reality, so simple that even earth worms can do them. So, stick with me. There's a bit of science to get through, but once you understand these techniques, you can use them on everything and everyone from pet rabbits to horses and spouses (often the hardest beast of all to train) with amazing success.

~

Operant conditioning is all about consequences. Indeed, if you want to distil the whole body of literature about operant conditioning into a single sentence it would be this: *The likelihood of a behaviour occurring again is increased or diminished depending on its consequences*. That is, if a behaviour results in a pleasant outcome it is more likely to be repeated. If a behaviour results in an unpleasant outcome it is less likely to be repeated.

Much of what we know about operant conditioning we learned from three key theorists: John Watson, Edward

Thorndike and B.F. Skinner. Although some of their research methods might now be considered old fashioned and even unethical (both Watson and Thorndike were born in the 1870s, while Skinner was born in 1904), they changed the way behaviour was thought about and studied, and their discoveries are still relevant today. More importantly, their findings have been verified and proven many times over by hundreds of researchers on many different species of animal since they were first discovered.

Watson, Thorndike and Skinner are considered the founders of the field of psychology known as behaviourism. Behaviourism changed the focus of psychological study from the mind to measurable and quantifiable behaviour, and is largely responsible for taking psychology out of the humanities and establishing it as a scientific discipline.

The school of behaviourism dominated psychology for several decades but began to fall out of favour in the 1970s for a few important reasons. Many people saw behaviourism as overly reductionist and mechanistic because it tried to explain all behaviour as a function of its consequences. Also, the fundamental behaviourist tenets seemed to be in direct conflict with Christian beliefs, because the behaviourist view that humans are driven by instincts and desires collides with the

Christian belief that humans, made in the image of God, have free will and can choose between right and wrong.

However, I think that where behaviourism fails is that it doesn't adequately acknowledge an animal's ethology. It's a great way of training behaviours, but the behaviours that it's possible to train are very much going to rely on the instincts, senses and abilities that the animal is born with. The easiest thing to train an animal to do is something it has evolved to do. This is both a hindrance and a benefit to trainers. The phenomenon was first discovered by two of Skinner's students (Breland and Breland) who wrote a paper titled 'The Misbehaviour of Organisms'. (Skinner's most famous paper was titled 'The Behaviour of Organisms', so the title was a little academic in-joke.) Breland and Breland had turned away from their lives as psychology researchers and started up an animal-training business based on the principles of behaviourism. But they ran into problems . . . they discovered that while in theory you can train an animal to do anything, in practice it is another story. You can train a pigeon to peck at a plastic disk to get some seed, but you can't train it to push the disk with its wing because it didn't evolve to push things with its wings. Breland and Breland trained a racoon to pick up coins and place them into a money box, but over time the racoon started spending more and more time rubbing the coins together. It would hold the coin in the slot of the money box but wouldn't let it go – instead, it would snatch it back and rub it with its hands. A pig trained to perform a similar task kept stopping to rub the disks it was supposed to drop against the ground. It eventually became so slow and the desired behaviour was reinforced so infrequently that it disappeared altogether. They called this 'instinctive drift', or the tendency for learned behaviours to drift towards the innate.

Scientist Richard Dawkins writes that humans evolved in 'middle earth', a place where things are big and small but not infinitesimally big or unimaginably small. Therefore, when it comes to imagining these things the human brain struggles. (They say if you understand quantum physics, you don't understand quantum physics.) Which makes me think that humans are just as predisposed to instinctive drift as non-human animals.

But I digress . . . Watson was responsible for the now-famous experiment in which he conditioned a nine-month-old child known as Little Albert to become frightened of a white rat by showing him the rat and, at the same time, making a loud clanging noise. Before the experiment, Little Albert enjoyed stroking and patting the rat, but afterwards, he would cry and try to escape when it was shown to him. Eventually his fear extended to other white furry things, including a researcher's fur collar and a Santa Claus beard.

Although this experiment may seem unethical today, Watson had demonstrated that natural human behaviour was easily modified via conditioning.

Will the real Little Albert please stand up?

The fate of the child known as Little Albert has been a source of interest for many psychologists since the experiment was conducted. Who was Little Albert and was he forever frightened of white furry objects? The search for the real Albert was complicated by the fact that Watson was dismissed from his position at the university shortly after the experiment. Not, as you might think, for traumatizing an innocent infant but for having an affair with the graduate student who assisted him during the experiment.

A few years ago it was claimed that Albert was actually Douglas Merrite, the son of a wet nurse at a nearby hospital. Sadly, Douglas died at the age of six from hydrocephalus, a build-up of fluid in the ventricles deep within the brain. More recently, though, it has been claimed that Albert was actually William Barger, who died in 2007 at the age of 87. Although researchers were unable to determine if Barger had maintained his fear of white rats, when questioned his niece told researchers that her uncle was very scared of dogs and remained so for his whole life.

As an animal trainer, I would also be interested to know how the behaviour of the rat (let's call him Little Barry) was changed by the experiment. The loud noise that frightened Little Albert would presumably have also frightened Barry. Did Barry become frightened of all small humans? And, like Albert, did he generalize this fear and extend it to things that resembled infants (for instance, things that smelled like mashed banana and milk vomit)?

Another aspect of the experiment of interest to animal trainers is the degree to which Little Albert extended the object of his fear to cover other white furry things. The flow-through effect of the white rat/furry collar/beard is highly adaptive. That is, it makes sense for humans and other animals to be frightened of things that are similar to other things that have frightened them in the past. If you have ever been bitten by a spider, you will probably be cautious about walking through all webs; you won't stop to try to determine the species from the shape of its web. This is called generalization and it explains why the horse that is badly frightened by a flapping bag can often extend that fear to towels, saddle blankets and even fly veils, despite never having had a frightening experience with those objects.

Edward Thorndike was the first researcher to systematically study operant conditioning. He put cats in boxes that they could only escape from if they pushed a lever or pulled a string. The hungry cats would try to escape the puzzle boxes to get a fish reward. Thorndike noted that the first time the cat was placed in the box it took a long time to work out how to escape, but subsequent trials became quicker until eventually the cats could escape almost immediately.

Thorndike wrote that over time the cats' behaviour became 'more orderly, more deliberate, more efficient', which is interesting because it is a good way to describe the difference between untrained and trained animals. Well-trained animals become less chaotic, less random and far quicker and easier to manage than their untrained counterparts.

He also noted that, statistically, it was obvious that the cats didn't suddenly have a moment of understanding; they simply practised a rewarded behaviour more frequently in the same position because the number of trials taken to escape predictably diminished. As evidence of this, Thorndike noted that when a cat that had previously escaped from a box by pulling a string was placed in a box that had no string, it would paw the air where the string might have been.

Thorndike also showed that watching an experienced cat escape from a box did not shorten the time required for an observer cat. Neither did manipulating the cat's limbs through the motion required. So, if Thorndike helped the cat escape by holding its paw and pulling the string, it didn't learn to escape any quicker than the cats that hadn't been helped.

Thorndike also did some experiments with other animals. He put chicks into small boxes and removed them as soon as they started pecking. Pretty soon the chicks would peck as soon as they were put into a box. He reasoned that this did not demonstrate 'understanding' but was simply a process of trial-and-error learning.

Two rules for learning

Out of his research Thorndike distilled two main rules for operant conditioning. These are just as important and relevant today as they were when the research was first conducted.

Repetition of a response strengthens it. That is, the more often a behaviour is performed, the more likely it is to be performed again.

Behaviours are either strengthened or weakened depending on their consequences. If the cat was able to escape and get the fish reward, the behaviour it performed just before it escaped would be more likely to occur again.

These rules are particularly useful to horse trainers because they encompass so much of what is important for us to remember every day. Every time the horse repeats a behaviour it is rehearsing it and getting better at it. Letting the horse practise an incorrect behaviour over and over again until the correct response is finally achieved in order to 'finish on a good note' is *not* a useful strategy, because in the process of achieving one good repetition the horse has practised many incorrect ones. It is far more useful to break down each training task into its smallest component parts and practise each part until the horse is very reliable. Achieving the correct behaviour can be very much like a seesaw. If the horse has practised a lot of incorrect responses, that's a lot of weight on one side of the seesaw. To balance it out and lift the good behaviour off the ground, you need a correspondingly large number of correct repetitions before the correct behaviour is reliable. When you are training a horse (or a dog, or a monitor lizard, etc.), your job is to put as much weight as possible on the correct end of the seesaw.

The second rule is also worth thinking about. It is the immediate consequences of a behaviour that matter — not what went before, or the long-term outcome, or what you believe the horse understands or the importance of the event . . . It simply comes down to what is reinforced and what isn't. By virtue of their evolution, horses (and other animals) are opportunists, not philanthropists. They will go to where the reinforcement is because it makes evolutionary sense to do so. The wonderful

Australian horseman Tom Roberts used to ask his students if a behaviour profited the horse or not. If a behaviour profits the horse because directly afterwards it receives a release of pressure, an ability to avoid work or scary things, freedom or a food reward, then it will be repeated. Praise, prizes and slaps on the neck do not profit the horse and therefore will not increase the likelihood of the behaviour occurring again.

~

B.F. Skinner is responsible for most of what we know today about operant conditioning. He determined that it is indeed the consequences of a behaviour that determine how likely it is that the behaviour will be repeated.

He invented the Skinner box (similar to Watson's puzzle box), a device that can be used to study conditioning by either rewarding or punishing various behaviours, such as key pecking for pigeons and lever pushing for rats. For example, if a rat brushed past a lever in the Skinner box, a pellet of food might drop into the feed container. The rats learned at a predictable rate to press the lever to obtain food.

Using the data he collected, Skinner determined that there are three types of responses (which he called operants) that can follow behaviour:

1. Neutral operants neither increase nor decrease behaviour. For example, if the rat pressed the wall next to the lever and nothing occurred, the lack of response would be deemed neutral as it neither increased nor decreased the behaviour.
2. Reinforcing operants (which can be either positive or negative) increase the likelihood that the behaviour will occur. If the rat pressed a lever and acquired food, this is a reinforcing operant and it would make the rat more likely to press the lever in future.
3. Punishing operants (which can also be either positive or negative) make it less likely that a behaviour will occur again. If the rat pressed the lever and received an electric shock it would be less likely to press the lever again in the future.

Skinner also discovered that when a behaviour that has previously been reinforced is no longer rewarded, it diminishes in frequency. This is called extinction. Interestingly, though, in more recent times researchers have used MRI to track brain activity and show that behaviours we consider extinct still exist in the brain, they are just suppressed. Building on this work, Joseph LeDoux showed that fearful behaviours are far more resistant to extinction than other behaviours, which is significant because scientist Janne Winther Christensen has shown that fearful behaviours are the major cause of horse/human accidents.

Although fear behaviours resist extinction, recent research into the pharmacological manipulation of memory formation has shown that administering a beta-blocker such as propranolol can disrupt the formation of long-term fear memories and make them less prone to retrieval. Beta-blockers act by blocking the effect of the stress hormones adrenaline and noradrenaline, which then slows heart rate and lowers blood pressure.

So what does this mean for the average horse owner? It means that during training and handling we need to avoid triggering fearful responses in the horse as much as possible. The research shows that horses don't 'get over' extremely fearful experiences; instead, they are stored in the brain and are far less subject to extinction than other behaviours. Introducing novel things very gradually and consolidating correct, trained responses both in hand and under saddle at every stage of the horse's training are important ways of reducing fear.

As we will discuss later, the amygdala (the canary in the coal mine when it comes to fear responses) is proportionately larger in the horse than in most other mammals. From the perspective of the horse's evolution this makes sense. The wild horse has just a few tricks up his sleeve when it comes to survival:

vigilance, speed, an ability to learn fast via classical conditioning and an almost perfect memory. However, for horse trainers this means that when the horse is frightened by something — for example, clippers — an indelible relationship between the clippers and fear can be created and stored in memory.

Sometimes the horse's fear seems almost feigned because to us it seems illogical. Some horses are terrified of clippers while others are untroubled by them, and for us humans it's hard to make sense of that because clippers are not deadly. But fear is not logical; it's physiological and biological. There are a multitude of human phobias and many appear to be completely illogical — unless of course the phobia is yours and then it is very real and very, very frightening. The best way to train the horse is to avoid fear in every situation. But once fearful behaviours have been learned, the best way to deal with them is with a correct training plan, empathy and patience.

I have a favourite way to train horses to approach objects they are frightened of. In our local area, rubbish collection day can be quite dynamic if you are trying to take a young horse for a quiet walk around the streets. We have large green wheelie bins and their shape and smell are so unlike anything the horse has already habituated to that they are quite terrifying (for both horse and rider). When the horse sees the first wheelie bin it will usually prick her ears, raise her head and neck, and slow her walk. This is the rider's cue to ride a downward transition to halt. It usually only takes fifteen or so seconds for the horse to change from fear to curiosity if an object isn't moving, so the rider should sit quietly and count to 20. Usually after 20 seconds the rider will notice that the horse's ears are not pinned quite as forward but occasionally one ear may flick back. Once this is happening the rider should quietly ask the horse for two steps forwards and then ride a downward transition to halt again. After another 20 seconds the process can be repeated, and so on until the horse has passed the bin. I don't ever expect the horse to touch the bin. I don't think touching makes them less scared of objects that they're frightened of. I mean, I don't really mind big, hairy spiders but I'd rather not pat one and I don't think it would make me like them more.

If you use this systematic approach for all scary objects, the horse is better able to visually process the object (after all, their distance vision has way less acuity than ours and their focal distance is much slower to change) and also any expressions of the flight response are corrected by the downwards transitions. The horse becomes less fearful over time because the training is clear and helps in the formation of consistent habits.

But back to Skinner. He maintained that the study of observable behaviour was more scientific than trying to study internal mental states. This is a really useful message for horse trainers dealing with problem behaviours, because while it is easy to try to rationalize the motivation for a horse's behaviour (for example, the horse doesn't like doing dressage), it's far more useful to examine what the horse does with his legs and body when developing a training solution. After all, it is impossible to truly know what the experience of another creature is. We cannot control the horse's brain (indeed, that would be ethically and morally wrong). All we can do is train his body to respond to our cues. As Andrew McLean once pointed out, when we train a horse (and any other animal), what we are actually doing is simply training muscles via tendons and ligaments to pull on bones.

I think it's useful to teach horse owners to describe their horse's problem behaviours purely as a function of the horse's legs – not of the horse's mind. Because it is in the description of what the horse's legs do that the training solution lies. I recently had a conversation with a student who told me that, at a recent dressage event, her horse was 'tense' and 'an idiot'. This description doesn't really offer any direction for future training but we were able to determine, eventually, that her horse had been inconsistent in both the rhythm of the footfalls and in maintaining line. This is where the solution lies. We cannot know or change the way the horse thinks, but we can assess and improve its training so that it is better able to cope with difficult situations.

As we've already discussed, one of Skinner's most important and, at the time, most revolutionary, discoveries was that behaviour is controlled by its consequences. That is, the strength and frequency of a behaviour is governed by what comes after it. If a behaviour results in a pleasant outcome, it is more likely to be repeated. If a behaviour results in an unpleasant outcome, it is less likely to be repeated. The operant conditioning grid below shows this basic principle in a pretty clear and easy-to-understand way. Of course, in real life nothing is quite as straightforward and simple as a neat diagram, and there is sometimes an inevitable blurring of the distinctions between the quadrants, but it serves as a useful starting point.

Skinner's operant conditioning quadrants

	Decrease Behaviour	**Increase Behaviour**
Add	Positive Punishment	Positive Reinforcement
Remove	Negative Punishment	Negative Reinforcement

Source: All positive Dog Training LLC.

Let's start by looking at both forms of reinforcement, as these are the most effective and ethical tools in the horse trainer's toolkit.

A note on the use of positive and negative . . . Psychology is a science, so when the terms positive and negative are used they mean adding and taking away, respectively. They are not value judgments about the ethics of using food rewards. Thus, in positive reinforcement something reinforcing is added after a behaviour (which increases the likelihood the behaviour will occur again), while in positive punishment something aversive is added after a behaviour (which will decrease the likelihood that the behaviour will occur again).

Positive reinforcement

This is adding something reinforcing (something that the horse seeks out, such as food and wither scratching) after a desirable behaviour in order to increase the likelihood of the behaviour occurring again. So, for example, if the horse walks up to the gate to be caught and you give him a handful of treats, he will be more likely to walk up to the gate in the future.

In training, we say that the reinforcement must be contingent upon the correct behaviour. This means that the reward must be delivered exactly as the horse does the thing you want him to do. If you give the horse a carrot after a ride, you are not reinforcing the ride. Instead, you are reinforcing whatever it was that the horse did just before the carrot went into his mouth.

For positive reinforcement to be effective we need to use a reinforcer — something the animal (or human) finds desirable. The value of a reinforcer can be measured only in terms of the degree to which it makes the behaviour more likely to occur in the future. So, if the rider yells 'Good boy!' at the top of their lungs and pounds the horse on the neck when he jumps the fence correctly, it is not likely to be reinforcing; however, a scratch on the withers might be very reinforcing. Good animal trainers watch their subjects to find out what stimuli *are* reinforcing and then use them, rather than deciding on a stimuli they *think* is reinforcing and using that.

Interestingly enough, palatable foods are more reinforcing if they are not part of the horse's everyday diet. (This is less likely in young horses, because they are often afraid of, and avoid, new things.) Horses that have been exposed to valued foods such as carrots and apples but do not receive them as part of their daily ration may perform with a higher consistency for apples and carrots than those that are fed them on a daily basis.

For trainers of other species, reinforcers may include toys (chew toys for dogs) and play, but horse trainers usually stick to food and tactile rewards. Patting is not reinforcing to horses as they do not pat each other in the herd. However, they do practise mutual grooming, most often focusing on the wither area.

Our praise and love are not reinforcers. If horses respond to words of praise such as 'good boy' it is because they have become associated with scratching or food rewards. The words 'good boy' precede and therefore start to predict the scratching, so they become a secondary or conditioned reinforcer, and something that is not inherently reinforcing becomes reinforcing. This association occurs because of classical conditioning.

Anyone who has ever handled stallions during breeding is aware of how strong secondary reinforcers can be. In the breeding season the equipment used (the stallion bit or head collar) and the environment (the serving yard or dummy) can become arousing (for the stallion, hopefully not the handler) because they precede a reinforcer (sex) and therefore become conditioned or secondary reinforcers. It can be a little bit disconcerting for stallion handlers when their charges all rush to the gate with erections if they see them carrying a bull bit. (Before laughing at how silly stallions are it is worthwhile thinking for an instant about human sexual response and just how much of it is also classically conditioned . . . in the next chapter we'll talk about the jar of pennies experiment.)

Horses have evolved to seek out food, so the appearance of dinner can be very exciting for them. The sound of dinner preparations and the arrival of the equipment used can become conditioned reinforcers. On large studs, where it can take many minutes for feed to arrive, you can often see some interesting behaviours that have been inadvertently reinforced. Pawing gates, striking the feed bin with their hooves, running the fence and even head nodding are behaviours that are often reinforced by the sight of the feed bucket (which has become a secondary reinforcer). I used to own a broodmare that urinated every time the feed trolley approached her paddock, probably because peeing had been inadvertently reinforced in the past.

I was once a supervisor for a Master's thesis investigating the Ponzo illusion. (On a page, two parallel lines of the same length will appear different lengths if converging lines are drawn through them.) As part of the research, we trained horses (using positive reinforcement) to pick various different arrangements of lines by touching their noses to laminated boards. When it was my turn to present the boards, I was distracted for a few seconds, missed the moment when the mare we were training touched the board but clicked a few seconds later when she was licking it. From that moment on she licked the boards every single time.

In a training context it can be difficult to deliver reinforcements at the correct time as there is an inevitable delay between the behaviour and the trainer's hand delivering the treat. This is why conditioned reinforcers are very useful. The conditioned reinforcer is usually a sound (such as a word or a click) that, when paired with a food reward, precisely marks the correct behaviour and gives the trainer a small window in which to deliver the reward. Conditioned reinforcers are a great addition to any horse trainer's tool kit. We will look at conditioned reinforcers in much more detail in the next chapter.

It's also worth pointing out here that human gamblers playing poker or slot machines are in the thrall of a variable schedule of positive reinforcement. And although the use of positive reinforcement has received a lot of interest in the popular press and on social media, it doesn't guarantee good training and doesn't release its practitioners from responsibility. It is not a magic pill that will solve all of an animal's problems. It should be applied judiciously and with the same acute attention paid to timing as negative reinforcement.

Negative reinforcement

Negative reinforcement involves removing something mildly annoying (such as rein or leg pressure) after a desirable behaviour in order to increase the likelihood of that behaviour occurring again — for example, when the rider applies pressure to the rein and the horse slows or stops, then the rider releases the pressure on the rein.

In my opinion, negative reinforcement is the most important yet most misunderstood of all the learning modalities. The misapplication of negative reinforcement has been shown to be at the root of most problem behaviours in the horse. There are a few rules to remember:

1. It is not the aid that trains the horse; it is the *release* of the aid that trains the horse. That is, it's not the rider's leg pressure that makes the horse go forward, it is the removal of the rider's leg pressure.

2. The release of the pressure must be contingent upon the correct behaviour. If the horse halts there must be a softening of the rein pressure. It's quite common to see horses that halt and then reef on the reins. This can be time-consuming to retrain but easy to (inadvertently) train. If the rider fails to release the pressure of the reins when the horse halts, the horse will occasionally reef at the bit, thus providing himself with a release of pressure, and therefore making the behaviour more likely to occur in future. Horses don't distinguish between 'bad' and 'good' behaviours, they repeat what is reinforced. Therefore, the horse that reefs on the reins is not being disobedient; it is simply repeating a behaviour that has been reinforced in the past. Famous animal trainer Bob Bailey says that you get the behaviour you reinforce,

not necessarily the behaviour you want. Rein reefing is a really good example of this.

3. The pressure used in negative reinforcement must start very lightly and escalate over a predictable timeframe. If the horse doesn't go forward from the rider's leg, the pressure of the leg must be incrementally increased and then removed the instant the horse goes forward. This is an aspect of negative reinforcement that is often overlooked, and it is one of the reasons it is an ethical training tool. When training is correct, the horse chooses the level of pressure at which she performs the behaviour. The horse can avoid uncomfortable pressure by going forward from very light leg pressure. This gives her a degree of control that is an important part of maximizing welfare.

4. Each aid must have only one response. If the horse is trained to go forward from leg pressure, then leg pressure must always mean go forward — it cannot also be used as an aid for anything else.

5. If intermittent pressures (such a whip taps or small heel kicks) are used there should be no gaps greater than a second between them or the horse will perceive the gap as a release of pressure.

Punishment

Now that we have looked at both forms of reinforcement we'll turn our attention to both forms of punishment. Punishment reduces the likelihood of behaviours occurring, which means it is not a great way to acquire new behaviours. After all, in the process of training the horse will quite often trial less-perfect forms of the desired behaviour, and this is good because it allows us as trainers to shape that behaviour, over time, into behaviours we want. For example, when you are loading a young horse into the float for the first time, you are asking him to do something completely new. The horse doesn't know that the task is to walk from the ground onto the ramp and into the float, but if the leading responses are well installed he will, with encouragement, take a single step onto the ramp. This is a good place to begin and if it is reinforced carefully at every step (with a release of the leading rein pressure and wither scratches/treats) the horse will soon learn to walk onto the float. The young horse that has a history of punishment will be hesitant to trial new behaviours because he has learned that some behaviours have really unpleasant consequences.

Punishment is problematic in a horse training environment because it assumes that the learner has the mental capacity to change its future behaviour in order to avoid consequences in the future. Not all humans can demonstrate this capacity. If punishment was an effective training tool there would be no such thing as repeat offenders in our jails and no one would ever receive more than one speeding fine.

Punishment is associated with certain mental states, such as fear and frustration, in the punished animal. Punishment decreases learning. Sigmund Freud pointed out (and it has since been verified) that while certain amounts of fear and frustration actually increase learning, large amounts suppress it. We learn best in a slightly heightened state of arousal, but once our adrenaline levels get to a certain point, learning speed decreases.

Animal behaviourist Daniel Mills summarized an array of problems associated with punishment. According to Mills, punishment:

- is non-directive; that is, it suppresses certain behaviours but does nothing to enhance desirable ones
- can desensitize the animal to the punishing stimulus if the intensity is not optimal
- carries the risk of causing emotional changes that can impede the rate at which new behaviours are learned, and may lower motivation to trial new responses
- may cause powerful fear associations between the punisher and the animal.

In horse training environments certain highly dangerous behaviours such as rearing and bucking *seem* to justify the use of punishment. This mindset is formed through the belief that the horse's misbehaviour is deliberate and that it is aware of its misdemeanours. Aside from the obvious welfare concerns associated with this belief, there are also other functional issues that may arise when punishment is employed.

Most misbehaviours that occur in a training context are flight-response related; that is, they are physical expressions of the horse's predator evasion repertoire such as bucking, shying and bolting. Using punishment in a situation where the horse has already reverted to the flight response is highly problematic because punishment increases levels of fear and frustration, and thus will probably only escalate the behaviour in the long-term. The desire to 'teach the horse a lesson' is a common one but has no place in a modern training environment.

The other problem with punishment is that it *must* be contingent upon the undesirable behaviour. That is, it must occur during the undesirable behaviour. If a trainer chooses to use punishment while a horse is bucking, the punishment must be delivered while the horse is bucking — which is almost impossible to do. If the punishment is delivered after the horse bucks, what the trainer is punishing is not the bucking but whatever behaviour is occurring after the bucking.

Quite probably what is being punished is normal movement. It is useful to remember that there is no such thing as a behavioural vacuum – the horse is never between behaviours. So punishment which is not contingent upon the undesirable behaviour is most likely contingent upon a desirable behaviour.

When animals are repeatedly exposed to painful stimuli they lose all control over their environment. If this is sustained and inescapable, a state called learned helplessness can set in. When an animal reaches a state of learned helplessness they no longer try to avoid painful stimuli; they simply give up and become dull.

Learned helplessness was first identified by Martin Seligman when he put puppies into a box that was divided by a low wall. When he electrified the floor of the box the puppies soon learned to jump over the low wall and escape the shocks. If he electrified both sides of the floor many of the puppies eventually gave up and lay on the floor whimpering. Even when the electrified floor was turned off the puppies remained dull and uninterested in their surroundings. Significantly, in later life the puppies that had developed learned helplessness in the first experiment would revert to a state of learned helplessness very quickly if exposed to punishment.

Later experiments have shown that it is the uncontrollable nature of the stimuli that interferes with subsequent avoidance learning. Animals that learn early on in their lives to put up with pain are subsequently more difficult to train, even when the training is correct. The symptoms of learned helplessness may include depression, anhedonia (the inability to find pleasure in normally pleasurable activities), and motivational, cognitive and emotional deficits.

Consider the difference between negative reinforcement and positive punishment. In negative reinforcement the horse can produce the behaviour at any point during the aversive stimulus. In punishment the onset of the aversive stimulus is unpredictable: it provides no behavioural solutions. Negative reinforcement gives the horse a degree of control over her environment because she can 'turn off' the aversive stimuli with her behaviour. Positive punishment gives him no such opportunities.

I'm not sure why punishment retains such a prominent place in popular training culture. It is ineffective, hard to administer and highly reinforcing for the punisher. If I have clients who are overly attached to the use of punishment during training I often suggest that they keep a journal of its use to determine if it is working. Punishment is defined by its effect; that is, that it decreases a behaviour. So, if a horse is being regularly punished and the behaviour isn't significantly diminished, then what is being administered is not punishment, it is abuse.

On being enough

The horse must always know that she is enough. She must know that she is trained enough, is strong enough and fit enough for the task. She did not choose you or ask to be ridden. She does not dream of glory or seek out fame. As riders, we borrow her speed and athletic ability. And we must pay for them with empathy, patience and consistent training.

Negative punishment

Negative punishment occurs when something that is reinforcing, such as food, is removed after an unwanted behaviour in order to reduce the incidence of that behaviour occurring again. It's what your parents were using when they took away your smartphone, sent you to your room or grounded you for misbehaving in class. They were removing reinforcing things (phones, freedom, social interaction) as a way of reducing your misbehaviour. It's often ineffective because it's usually delayed and not contingent upon the incorrect behaviour.

One of the most common problems people ask me about is the horse that is difficult to catch. If you take your horse from the paddock you are removing it from food, freedom and friends. This is negative punishment, which reduces the likelihood of behaviour occurring again, and it is therefore not surprising that horses will often resist being caught. It is useful to counteract this effect by clearly and regularly reinforcing the act of being caught with either wither scratching or treats.

It may seem like old news to look at the work of researchers who studied behaviour in the last century, but it's worth remembering that over 2000 years ago a Greek librarian called Eratosthenes calculated the Earth's circumference with remarkable accuracy using two sticks. And, just like the work of Eratosthenes, which has been shown many times over to be valid, the work of Watson, Thorndike and Skinner has also been shown to be both scientifically valid and relevant in a modern setting.

7.

CLASSICAL CONDITIONING

The story of Clever Hans is not just the story of an old man and a horse. It's the story of a fascinating form of learning known as classical conditioning. Both humans and animals learn with classical conditioning and most of the time we're not even aware that we're doing it. Classical conditioning is responsible for the sense of wellbeing you get when you smell a loved one's perfume, and also for the nausea you feel when you taste the cheap chardonnay on which you once overindulged. It can spike your insulin levels and spur on your immune system and yet its discovery was almost accidental and was made, not by a psychologist, but by a physiologist called Ivan Pavlov.

The eldest of eleven children, Pavlov joined the seminary after finishing school in order to become a Russian Orthodox priest like his father, but his burning intellectual curiosity eventually drove him to swap the priesthood for life as a scientist.

Pavlov's scientific output was extensive, and he was nominated for the Nobel Prize four times before finally winning it in 1904 for his work on the physiology of digestion. He worked for many years as head of the physiology department at the Institute of Experimental Medicine in St Petersburg, and it was here that he conducted his now famous experiments. During his career, Pavlov attracted the attention and praise of Lenin, the head of the Soviet government, and he was enthusiastically supported by the Communist Party despite making no secret of his disdain for communist doctrine.

Pavlov made his accidental discovery while studying the production of saliva in dogs. He surgically implanted tubes into his research dogs' mouths so that he could measure how much saliva was produced when they ate powdered meat. However, Pavlov's experiment was complicated by the dogs' anticipation. Pavlov had an assistant who, each day, would bring the meat into the laboratory on a trolley that had a squeaky wheel. Pretty soon, when the dogs heard the squeaking they would begin to salivate — thus ruining Pavlov's experiment.

Pavlov was an intensely curious man and he began to explore this strange phenomenon. He rang a bell before the meat arrived and pretty soon the dogs, without any food, would begin to salivate at the sound of the bell. He repeated the same experiment with several different sounds and successfully conditioned the dogs to salivate at the sound of a tuning fork, an electronic buzzer and a metronome. Today we know this phenomenon as classical conditioning and it is an extremely important and powerful form of learning for both humans and animals. In classical conditioning, two stimuli are paired and a response, which initially could only be elicited by the second stimulus, is eventually able to be elicited by the first.

Let's look at that idea in a little more detail. In Pavlov's experiments the dogs were shown to salivate when presented with powdered meat. The meat was what is known as an unconditioned stimulus, and the salivation an unconditioned response, because they had not been classically conditioned. The sound of the bell was repeatedly paired with the meat, and when it was able to elicit salivation on its own, it became a conditioned stimulus. In this context the salivation then became a conditioned response.

Pavlov's classical conditioning

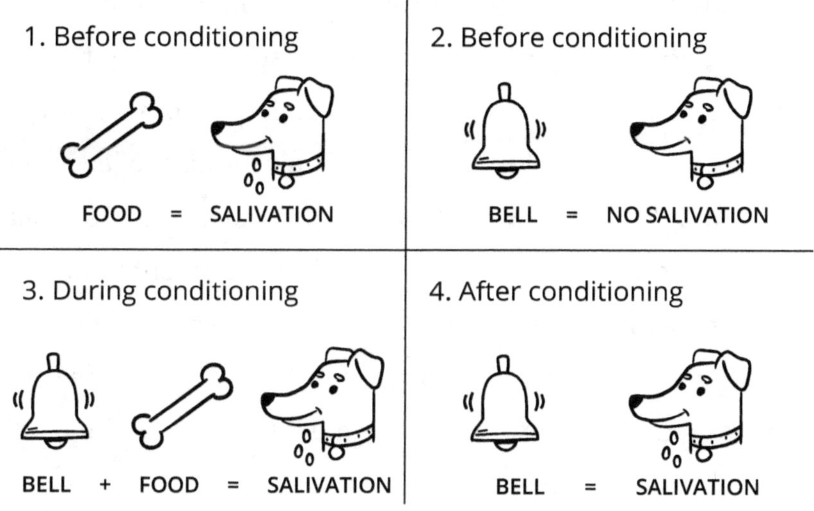

In later experiments Pavlov paired a mild electrical shock with the meat and, eventually, when the dogs were given a shock they would salivate. Interestingly, once the dogs began to salivate reliably when shocked, the shock appeared to be far less painful than before. We now call this counter conditioning, a form of learning used every day by animal trainers and human psychologists. In counter conditioning the conditioned stimulus is either unpleasant or painful (the electric shock) but when paired with an unconditioned stimulus that is desirable (the meat), the conditioned response (salivation) will still occur.

Because salivation is incompatible with fearful behaviour the dogs became less scared and showed less pain.

Counter conditioning is often used by animal trainers and zookeepers when performing unpleasant or mildly painful management and medical procedures, like clipping or giving needles, and in human psychology it forms the basis of cognitive behavioural therapy, a treatment for phobias and insomnia. In one of the most well-known early experiments done on counter conditioning, a young boy who was terrified of rabbits was allowed to eat his favourite food when sitting in the same room as a rabbit in a cage. He became less scared of the rabbit over time and was eventually able to pat it.

Classical conditioning, however, is not just a way of training animals and curing phobias. It is part of the placebo effect, a phenomenon in which the beneficial effect of a 'pretend' treatment is caused by the patient's expectations. So powerful is the placebo effect that trials for new drugs always include a control group of patients who are not given the new drug but instead are unknowingly given harmless and ineffective sugar pills. Interestingly, in many studies the group of patients given the placebo treatment also shows an improvement in their condition. That is why many people define medicine as any treatment that is more effective than a similarly administered placebo.

Some people ascribe the placebo effect to a patient's positive mindset, but it is more than just that because it also occurs in animals. Scientists Ader and Cohen discovered that the immune system can be classically conditioned. Their subjects were a strain of laboratory mice prone to the autoimmune disease lupus. The mice were given a uniquely flavoured drink just before being injected with cyclophosphamide, a powerful immune-suppressing drug used to treat lupus. Several days later the mice were given the same flavoured drink and some were also given cyclophosphamide, while others were given a placebo. Interestingly enough, the mice given the placebo also showed a considerable reduction in their symptoms — almost as though they had been given the treatment. Subsequent studies have shown that classical conditioning can both increase and suppress immune function depending on which drug the novel-tasting drink is paired with.

Classical conditioning explains many aspects of our behaviour. It is why when you are sick after eating a certain food you will go to great lengths to avoid that food in the future. This is called conditioned taste aversion and it is highly adaptive as it would have helped our ancestors avoid eating poisonous or spoiled food. Scientists have demonstrated conditioned taste aversion in rats after only one trial. In these experiments, thirsty rats were allowed to drink sweet, flavoured water and 75 minutes later they were injected with a drug that causes nausea. A few days later, even after being deprived of water for the previous 24 hours, the rats avoided the flavoured water. Interestingly, though, if the rats were shocked (instead of being given the drug that causes nausea) they did not show any taste aversion. They also did not form an aversion to the physical appearance of food even if it made them nauseous. Birds, however, have been shown to rapidly form aversions to the appearance of food and this is almost certainly because they rely more on their sense of sight than on their sense of smell when identifying food. This has been exploited by some insect species that have evolved the same colouring as poisonous insects to make themselves less attractive to birds.

Conditioned taste aversion has also been successfully exploited to train freshwater crocodiles to avoid eating poisonous cane toads. The cane toad was introduced into Australia to eat the cane beetles that were decimating sugar cane crops. Finding itself very much at home in its new environment, the toad has multiplied and spread out of control. Not only does it compete with native species for resources, it also contains a toxin which can kill native animals if eaten. Rangers have successfully trained crocodiles and other reptiles such as monitor lizards to avoid eating cane toads by killing toads, removing the poisonous organs from their bodies and injecting the carcasses with lithium chloride (a drug that causes intense nausea). When the crocodiles eat the poisoned toads they become nauseous and in one trial learned to avoid them in future.

Classical conditioning occurs unconsciously and, therefore, if you want to put an unconscious behaviour such as salivation on cue it's the only form of conditioning that will work. Lots of our physiological responses can be classically conditioned. New mothers with breastfeeding babies can attest to this. When I had young babies I learned that the milk let-down response often occurs after the classically conditioned cue of a baby's cry. It doesn't even have to be your own baby's cry (embarrassingly); it can be a random stranger's baby at the supermarket... I have a friend who was unable to breastfeed her newborn baby so she purchased a breast pump to express milk. For her, the sound of a baby crying did not elicit let-down but (you guessed it) the sound of the breast pump turning on did. It's not just human lactation, either, that can be conditioned. A few years ago, I was part of a project to test if camel mothers would let down milk without their calves, as it's mostly believed that they won't. Though it was a very small-scale project it quite clearly showed that replacing the classically conditioned cue of the camel calf with another classically conditioned cue would definitely elicit milk let-down.

Classical conditioning also plays a large role in sexual responses in both humans and animals. My partner and I used to live on a large thoroughbred stud (you're probably wondering where this anecdote is going). One of my partner's tasks was to control the stallions when they were serving mares. The stallions all lived in large, individual paddocks attached to a common laneway. When he walked along the laneway carrying the bridle used for serving, the stallions would all rush to their gates with erections. And human sexual response is just as prone to classical conditioning. Scientists have been able to condition human males to become sexually aroused at the sight of a jar of pennies simply by pairing the jar with erotic videos — that is, presenting the jar of pennies then pornography, jar of pennies then pornography. I'm no psychologist but as an animal trainer I think it's quite possible that classical conditioning is at the heart of human sexual fetishes. If the object of desire (let's say feet) was paired with the sight of something arousing, then it is quite likely that in the future the sight of feet could elicit sexual arousal. All thanks to classical conditioning.

Classical conditioning allows the horse to make predictions about future events because of the sequence of the stimuli; that is, if A occurs, B will follow. Second order or higher order conditioning occurs when the conditioned stimulus is preceded and thus paired with another stimulus. For example, if Pavlov had played a flute before ringing the bell and then feeding the dogs, the flute would eventually have elicited the salivating. Horses form higher order conditioning chains consisting of many stimuli. For example, when they are waiting to be fed sometimes just the sight of the feed shed door opening can elicit excitement when it is only the first in a long sequence of events that occurs before feeding.

In horse training, classical conditioning is inevitable, as horses are very quick to pair two stimuli. The rider's voice aids are trained via classical conditioning. If the rider says 'whoa' and then applies pressure on the reins, the correctly trained horse will slow or stop. Eventually, when the horse hears the command 'whoa' she will slow or stop without pressure on the reins because the rein pressure has become a conditioned response. The rider's seat and weight aids are also trained via classical conditioning. If the rider adopts a certain posture before performing a movement (which has been trained using operant conditioning), the horse will soon learn that the subtle change in posture precedes and therefore predicts the movement.

Pairing and piggybacking

The untrained horse will not learn to stop with just the word 'whoa' in the same way that Pavlov's dogs would never have salivated if he had simply rung the bell and never paired the sound with meat. It was the pairing of the bell and the powdered meat that made the bell effective, just as, in horse training, it is the pairing of the word 'whoa' and the slowing signals of the reins that causes the slowing to occur. In a sense, the aids or cues we train via classical conditioning piggyback onto the behaviours that we train via operant conditioning. This is why it is pointless for instructors to tell their students to 'use their seat' if the operantly trained responses are not already well established and reliable or the connection between the seat and the operantly trained response is not clear. The seat has no magical properties; it simply becomes a classically conditioned cue.

The effects of classical conditioning during training should never be underestimated. The amygdala is a part of the brain that plays a significant role in the processing of fearful emotions — it is almost like a gatekeeper for fear. The horse has the biggest amygdala of all the large domestic mammals, as fear-related responses are highly adaptive in prey species. When the horse suffers fear or pain during training, the behaviours he learns will have powerful fear associations. So if the horse is frightened during his early jumping lessons, that fear will be very difficult to eradicate because fearful behaviours in the horse are resistant to extinction. This is one of the many reasons why it is very important to keep trainees (whether human or animal) calm and happy during any form of learning.

It is also important to understand that classical conditioning will not occur if the stimuli are presented in the incorrect order. If Pavlov had given the dogs their powdered meat before ringing the bell, they would not have learned to salivate when the bell was rung. Similarly, if Pavlov had decided, once the dogs were conditioned to salivate at the sound of a bell, to also do a dance while ringing the bell the dogs would not have learned to salivate when Pavlov danced because the effect of the dancing would have been blocked by the existence of the previously learned stimuli — the bell. This effect is, unsurprisingly, called blocking and it occurs when previous learning interferes with learning a new stimulus.

Another important aspect of classical conditioning to understand is overshadowing, which occurs when two stimuli are presented at the same time. The subject will only react to the most noticeable (salient) stimuli. For example, if you are teaching a dog to sit you might think that the word 'sit' is the most salient part of the cue. But if, when you say sit, you also lean forward towards the dog, wave your hand and put your other hand in your pocket, the word sit might be overshadowed by the movement of your body. If you then try to get the dog to sit when you are sitting down on the couch, the word sit may not be a reliable cue because the most salient part of the cue (the movement of your body) is missing.

Extinction

Classical conditioning is a very powerful form of learning but it is not necessarily infallible. Pavlov discovered that if he rang the bell several times without giving the dogs any meat, the rate at which they salivated would diminish. This is called extinction and while it may look as though the subject has forgotten their previous training, it's not quite as simple as that. Studies show that neurons in the brain still fire when the old cue is given, which suggests that extinction is a form of behavioural repression. The cue still exists but in a dormant state. This helps explain the phenomenon of spontaneous recovery, when a behaviour that has been extinguished suddenly returns at full strength. Spontaneous recovery is very important for horse trainers to understand because the horse is capable of learning behaviours after only one repetition, particularly if that behaviour involves the flight response. This ability has an adaptive function, as our horse's wild ancestors would not have had many second chances when it came to running away from predators. The more a horse practices a certain behaviour, the longer the behaviour will take to extinguish, and the more it will be prone to spontaneous recovery.

Here's an example. Harry was a large crossbred horse that had learned to buck during his early training. Eventually his owners decided that his behaviour would never change and he was sold to the rodeo, where he was used in saddle bronc competitions. For several years, Harry bucked wildly every time he was ridden and was reinforced by the rider falling off. However, as he grew a little older there were occasionally riders that he could not buck off and eventually he stopped bucking. A horse trainer who knew Harry through the rodeo bought him and finished his under-saddle training and, because he was tractable and calm, sold him to the local mounted police force. For three years, Harry was the ideal police mount — calm and steady. However, one night when he was on patrol he was startled by a crowd of people and he started bucking wildly, just as he had during his days in the rodeo, until his rider fell off. Everyone was very surprised that Harry had started bucking, but once you know a little about classical conditioning and spontaneous recovery it is not surprising at all.

The Rescorla-Wagner model and conditioned reinforcement

If we think about Pavlov's famous experiments we might wonder why the dogs learned to salivate when the bell was rung. What about the other stimuli in the room? The experiments were all conducted in Pavlov's laboratory by Pavlov himself so there were other stimuli that could have triggered the dogs' salivation. Why didn't the sight of Pavlov's hair/lab coat/shoes/briefcase also trigger the salivation?

The Rescorla-Wagner model explains why the bell became the conditioned stimulus because it demonstrates that the bell was both reliable and salient. That is, the bell was always present in exactly the same form and it was easy for the dogs to notice it because there were no other bells ringing in the laboratory. It's not necessary to be able to apply the Rescorla-Wagner model in order to become a good horse trainer, but it is interesting to note that the probability of behaviour can be modelled mathematically, as seen below.

Mathematical representation of the Rescorla-Wagner model

$$\Delta \underline{V}_{\underline{n}} = \underline{K}(\lambda - V_{n-1})$$

ΔV	Change in associative sterngth to CS_A
V_{AX}	Current associative strength to $CS_{A,X}$(context)
α_A	Salience of CS_A
β	Salience of UCS used in the Experiment
λ	Maximum associative strength possible

Because classical conditioning allows animals (and humans) to make accurate predictions about the world, it enables the use of a training device known as a conditioned reinforcer. If an animal hears a distinctive noise before being given a food reward, the two things will become paired and the distinctive noise can be used to mark correct behaviours with far more accuracy than delivering the food directly to the animal's mouth.

The potential for conditioned reinforcers in animal training was first exploited commercially by dolphin trainers, who noticed that the dolphins they were teaching to jump were, over time, doing smaller, faster and flatter jumps in order to get back to the side of the tank and receive their fish reward. The trainers needed a way to reward the dolphins at a distance, so they paired the sound of a whistle with a fish reward and soon they were able to reward the dolphins at a distance. This is why you will often see marine mammal trainers with whistles in their mouths. The whistle is not there to give the animal a cue; it is a way of rewarding behaviour.

Conditioned reinforcers are now used by animal trainers all over the world. Any distinctive sound can be used as a conditioned reinforcer, even a word spoken in a distinctive tone can be used — though this can take a little longer to establish as the animal has almost certainly heard many words throughout its lifetime, which will reduce the word's salience. The most well-known conditioned reinforcer used in animal training is a clicker, a small plastic box that produces a loud click when pushed. The sound of the clicker is both reliable (it's always the same) and salient (it's a very unusual sound), both of which make it very effective.

When creating the initial pairing between the click and food, it is important that very little time elapses between the two. Half a second is ideal in the beginning, though as training becomes more established it is possible to let a little bit more time elapse. Pavlov called this phenomenon the law of temporal contiguity — the fact that learning will not occur if there is too much time between the conditioned reinforcer and the reinforcing stimulus (usually food).

The anticipation of reinforcement that occurs when using a conditioned reinforcer stimulates dopamine pathways in the brain. Dopamine is a hormone and neurotransmitter that assists with many functions, including movement and pleasure, but more importantly for animal trainers it confers a degree of motivational salience — the cognitive (thinking) process that guides attention and motivation. Which basically means that the anticipation of reinforcement stimulates the beneficial production of dopamine which, in turn, increases the motivation to complete a task.

I have been incredibly lucky throughout my career to meet people who are passionate about training the animals in their care in the best possible way. Recently, a very talented local falconer and friend of mine developed a project to rehabilitate peregrine falcons and return them to the wild. Peregrines are quite simply the most extraordinary birds on the planet. The fastest animal ever, they can reach speeds of over 200 kilometres (124 mi) per hour and some of their adaptations (such as the baffles in their nasal cavity that allow them to breathe at unbelievably high speeds) have been used in the designs of military aircraft such as the stealth bomber.

The majority of juvenile peregrines do not survive their first winter. They are found by members of the public tired, cold and half-starved, and handed into rescue organizations. However, putting them in an aviary and feeding them isn't the best way to prepare them for release as they need to be fit and strong. This is where the skills of traditional falconers come in. If these juveniles are flown as part of their rehabilitation they stand a much better chance of long-term survival.

The most successful wild peregrines learn that the best way to use their extraordinary speed is to get as high as possible and stoop down on smaller birds from above. But getting a rehab bird to learn that skill isn't always straightforward. Right now, there is a project running testing the use of a conditioned reinforcer (a tiny beeper attached to the bird's back on a super-light backpack) to train the birds to fly high in order to get a beep and then a reward. It's never been documented before and there will, inevitably, be a delay between the beep and the reward but it's incredibly exciting to combine modern technology and the ancient art of falconry.

'Uhuh': the no-reward marker

Classical conditioning is amazing. It will form a connection between two stimuli as long as one precedes the other in quite quick succession. This is because mammalian brains are in many ways prediction machines. They are extremely adept at learning that if A occurs, B will follow. This is why a conditioned reinforcer works so well, because the animal learns that the click or the whistle precedes and therefore predicts the food. A stimulus can become a conditioned punisher, too. Sadly, this is why so many horses are frightened of whips.

It is also possible to train a conditioned no-reward marker (NRM), which is a signal the trainer uses to indicate that the animal's current course of action is not going to achieve a reward. For example, if you are training a horse to touch a large ball with her nose but she paws the ball instead, you could say 'uhuh' to indicate that a different behaviour is needed. Then, when she performs a behaviour that is more like touching, you would reinforce that.

The NRM is most effective if used very sparingly and in a situation where the horse is likely to immediately trial a more correct form of the behaviour. Used too often, it will either create frustration and anxiety or will simply fade into white noise. Used judiciously it can change a horse's course of behaviour and make the desired behaviour more obvious.

One of the world's leading animal trainers, Bob Bailey, is famous for saying that, as animal trainers Pavlov is always on our shoulder. What he means is that classical conditioning is an inevitable part of every training scenario even if we don't mean it to be. Within his lifetime, Pavlov could not possibly have known just how significant classical conditioning would be. And I doubt he could have imagined how his accidental discovery would come to be used by trainers and psychologists all around the world.

As for Pavlov, he spent 45 years as the head of physiology at the Institute of Experimental Medicine in St Petersburg which, with his guidance, became one of the most respected centres of learning in Russia. He was generous with his time and knowledge and throughout his career he held regular Wednesday meetings for students and staff, where they would gather and discuss different topics in an informal setting. He was also a brilliant scientist right to the end. When, at the age of 86, he lay dying of pneumonia he asked one of his students to sit by his bed in order to document the process in the hope that someday it would be useful. And although he had once wanted to become a priest, Pavlov died a firm atheist.

8.

HABITUATION, SHAPING AND WELFARE

The last forms of learning we're going to discuss are habituation and its mirror image twin, sensitization. These are what are known as non-associative forms of learning because (unlike operant conditioning and classical conditioning) they don't involve pairing a stimulus with a behaviour.

Habituation occurs when the response to a stimulus diminishes after repeated exposure to it. Basically, it is getting used to things. It is why people who live next to airports can sleep through the noise of aircraft taking off, and why young horses stop reacting to the saddle when trained correctly.

Almost everything in the animal kingdom can learn to habituate. Even the small worm *Caenorhabditis elegans* (loved by researchers from many fields because of its simple structure and very short life cycle) can be habituated to the noise of a researcher tapping a petri dish with their finger. This is pretty amazing considering this small worm has only 302 neurons in its nervous system, whereas humans have over 100 billion.

Some stimuli are hard to habituate to, especially if they are:

- too strong (for example, an electric fence)
- new (pigs)
- too close (clippers in the ears)
- appear suddenly (pedestrians with umbrellas)
- move erratically (a six-year-old child in a lion suit).

Habituation can be done gradually or all at once. When it is done all at once it is known as flooding. In humans, flooding is a psychotherapeutic technique where, for example, the person who is claustrophobic is made to stay in a small, confined space until their fear response diminishes. As someone who suffers from mild claustrophobia, the thought of this treatment makes my palms sweat. The treatment can be effective but it can also go completely wrong, causing massive anxiety and making the subject far more reactive in the presence of the stimulus. Humans who subject themselves to flooding techniques to cure phobias have the mental capacity to choose their own treatment and understand that the long-term gain is worth the short-term agony. Horses and other animals are unable to understand what is going on and therefore flooding should never be a part of any ethical training regime.

As an aside, when I discuss habituation with my university class I tell them about a treatment for arachnophobia that involves the subject being enclosed in a glass box (uncomfortably similar in shape to a coffin), the lid of which is then sprinkled liberally with live spiders. As part of this lecture I have a photograph of a tarantula which, I have to admit, is quite large when shown on the screen of a lecture theatre, and over the years I have had several students run out of the room when the spider appeared. Which just goes to show the power of fear, even in creatures that are able to reason.

Habituation is most rapid when expressions of the flight response are reduced throughout the duration of the habituation process. The most extreme example of this is the wheat box experiment that was documented by animal behaviourist Temple Grandin. In this experiment, a completely wild mustang was totally immobilized in a large box full of wheat (only its head and neck were free of the box) and then exposed to different scary stimuli such as brushes and flapping saddle cloths. Habituation to the scary stimuli occurred very rapidly.

However (and this is a big however), in my opinion there is a fine line between habituation and learned helplessness.

How do we know that in this situation the horse is habituating and not entering a state of learned helplessness? Horses react to fearful things by running away; it's a fundamental part of what makes the horse a horse. Completely taking away their ability to move must be terrifying. While I believe there are important lessons to be learned from the wheat box — namely that a reduction in movement of the horse's legs facilitates a more rapid habituation — the risks of learned helplessness are too great. The same applies to other methods that involve immobilization, such as hobbling the front legs: there is just too much risk of inducing indelible changes in the brain.

Over the years I've seen quite a few horses that have been trained to habituate to fearful stimuli using complete immobilization. This is often seen as a quick fix, a way of desensitizing the horse by either tying up both front and hind feet or by forcing the horse to lie down using ropes. For a certain period of time these horses can show remarkably little response to fearful stimuli such as flapping bags. Indeed, they show disturbingly little response to almost everything. However, this reaction is almost always, in my experience, temporary. One day the horse that appeared to be completely habituated to huge, wildly flapping bags will see the corner of a small, seemingly inoffensive bag and panic. Retraining these horses is a lengthy and time-consuming process, and the quick-fix training solution can take years to rectify.

Slowly does it

One of the most important things to remember when introducing any novel stimuli is that it must be introduced at the lowest possible threshold. If, for example, you turn on the clippers right next to the horse and they have a strong fear reaction, what you have taught them is that clippers are scary. Horses learn fear responses in just one repetition so you then have that memory of fear to contend with. It's far more efficient whenever possible to habituate the horse so slowly and carefully that no fear responses are ever shown.

There are a few commonly used evidence-based desensitization techniques but the caveat is the same for all of them: introduce the object to be habituated to at such a low threshold that there is no fear shown at all.

Counter conditioning is a very effective way to desensitize humans and non-humans to things that might scare them. As the name suggests, counter conditioning occurs when we change an aversive stimulus into a pleasing one. So, if we turn on the clippers and then feed the horse, the sound of the clippers will become a conditioned reinforcer that precedes and therefore predicts the arrival of food.

Counter conditioning is most often used as a way of getting animals to submit to necessary but uncomfortable therapeutic interventions such as injections. It's always a good idea to do this training before it is needed, because there are three things in life that are certain: death, taxes and vet bills. I usually use a conditioned reinforcer such as a clicker to make this process even more clear for the horse. Plus, because of the anticipation, the use of a conditioned reinforcer has the added bonus of some dopaminergic effects.

Getting a horse used to needles ideally takes two handlers. Handler one will hold the horse and handler two will hold the syringe and the clicker. While the horse is standing comfortably, handler two will present the syringe at such a distance that the horse shows no reaction, and will then click/treat. If the horse moves it should be stepped backwards quietly and firmly. However, it is much better if the process is done so gradually that the horse doesn't show any reaction at all. It is very easy to inadvertently reward a fear reaction by clicking and treating when the horse reacts to the needle. So it's important only to reward no reaction.

Gradually (over a number of sessions), the horse will be rewarded for standing still while the syringe is brought closer, then while the skin is swabbed, then while the needle's tip is placed against the skin. It's neither ethical nor necessary to give injections as part of training, but when it is necessary to give an injection the process should be repeated and then after the injection is given the horse should be rewarded for standing still. In this way the horse will associate the sight and smell of a syringe with a tasty and delicious treat, and not only will injections be easier to give, but they will be far less stressful for the horse too.

I recently used counter conditioning to retrain a gypsy cob mare that had become aggressive to saddle. Although only small, these nuggetty little horses are quite heavy and the sight of one launching at you with what appears to be intent to kill is quite disconcerting.

Behaviours often become emancipated from their cause – this means that even if the initial cause of the behaviour disappears, the behaviour still persists. The very well-meaning and experienced owner of the cob explained to me that the mare had first shown aggressive behaviour when she had gastric ulcers, and that although the mare's ulcers were now long gone, it was still dangerous to saddle her. This despite spending many thousands of dollars and two years trying to cure the behaviour with everything from saddle fit to hormones. The owner was just about to give up her dreams of riding this lovely little horse when she eventually saw a vet who, after an extensive physical examination, suggested that the problem was behavioural.

A very good friend of mine says that some horses are geniuses when it comes to solving pressure problems (I'm looking at you, thoroughbreds and Arabs) and some are geniuses when it comes to solving food problems. Almost all the cobs I've worked with have a tendency to become overweight, so they are constantly on diets and therefore are absolute geniuses when it comes to solving problems for food. Luckily for us the mare was no exception.

We used the same 'approach from a distance' technique that I described for the injections, but with a third person holding the saddle. We started with the saddle holder at least 20 metres (22 yd) away, which was where we estimated the mare would show no reaction. Gradually, the saddle holder was able to move closer a step at a time, stopping every step so I could click and reward the mare standing quietly without her ears back. As the saddle holder got closer the mare was more inclined to put her ears back, but the handler just stepped her quietly backwards while the saddle holder maintained the same distance between herself and horse. This is so the ears-back behaviour didn't remove the saddle, which would therefore inadvertently negatively reinforce the ears back. As soon as the mare stood quietly with relaxed ears I would click and reward.

Within about half an hour the mare was standing quietly while the saddle holder approached and carefully placed the saddle on her back. However, while it looked a bit like a miracle cure it really is just the first step of a long retraining journey. We were lucky: we were able to do the initial training in a place unfamiliar to the mare. Because horses are contextual learners, it would have been much more difficult if we'd had to do the first sessions in the place where the behaviour had been most often practised. Also, for two years the mare had been able to remove the saddle by putting her ears back and lurching at the trainer, so this behaviour had been reinforced many, many times. The road ahead is long but the owner is committed and very empathetic so I am confident we will eventually achieve a good result.

When I was talking to the owner before our training session she said, 'She's always been a bit tricky to saddle up. She moves around while you're trying to put the saddle on.' And this reminded me that in some ways our training is a dam wall that holds back a lot of unwanted behaviours, most of them related to the flight response. If a certain behaviour is not well trained it can act as a small breach in the wall. Over time this small breach can become a huge crack and the flight response behaviours can come flooding out. I think it is our duty as horse owners to identify these breaches and rectify them with training, not only for our own convenience and safety but also for the welfare of the horse.

Park

Standing still, or *park*, is probably the most important behaviour to train on the ground. As well as being extremely useful for situations like grooming, saddling, shoeing and mounting, it is a good way to test the horse's training and a great way to train the horse to self-regulate.

Start by ensuring the horse is able to step back quietly from light pressure on the lead rope (pressed towards his chest). This is the operantly conditioned foundation for the whole behaviour, so spend as much time as it takes to make this light and reliable. The backwards step must occur from the lead rope pressure and not from you stepping towards the horse or from waggling the lead rope, or from a voice command. Unless you are trying to get a reflex or an unconscious behaviour (like salivation or increased heart rate) under stimulus control, the first phase of training a behaviour is almost always operant conditioning.

Once the horse can step backwards from a light cue you can add a voice command. You might, for example, use the word 'back' and immediately afterwards step the horse backwards. Repeat until as soon as you say 'back' the horse steps backwards. It's useful to repeat this in the same place, as horses are very good at context-specific learning. You can usually tell that the process of classical conditioning is beginning because you'll see the horse's pectoral (chest) muscles twitch when you give the voice cue.

A couple of things to remember when you're training voice cues . . . They're not permanent. You'll have to continue to reinforce the connection between the voice and the stepping back periodically as the connection tends to fade over time. Also, if the behaviour fails, check the operantly conditioned foundation first. And remember the cue is 'back' (or whatever you choose) not, 'Back! Back! Get back you silly bugger. Back back back back back.'

Once you can do step-backs from a voice cue you can begin to train park. Face the horse, give a visual cue for park (I usually raise my hand, palm facing the horse) and take a step backwards. When the horse follows, immediately step him backwards to the place where he began. The quicker you can return the horse to his original starting place, the quicker he will learn to park. When you can take one backward step away from the horse, add another and so on until you can go to the full length of the lead rope without him following. Then you can add sideways steps (as though the horse was lunging you). *Pro-tip: begin sideways steps by going to the horse's off side, as he is much more accustomed to following you when you are on his near side.*

Your goal is to be able to walk a semi-circle at the full length of the lead rope while the horse stands quietly. Park is particularly powerful as a training tool because it teaches the horse to keep his legs still, even when he wants to move. The flight response is coupled to the movement of the horse's legs so, as well as being useful for shoeing, rugging, saddling and mounting, park is a great way of relaxing the horse.

Approach conditioning exploits the fear-reducing quality of actively chasing something scary.

It requires two handlers, one for the horse and one for the scary object. If the horse takes a step towards the scary object and the object moves away, the horse has learned how to make the thing it is frightened of go away. If you think this sounds a little like a form of operant conditioning, you're absolutely right. It's negative reinforcement. The horse removes the scary object by stepping towards it.

A friend of mine had a horse that was terribly frightened of bikes and we used approach conditioning to successfully desensitize it. She rode the horse and I rode a bike. We started at a distance of about 20 metres (22 yd) and as the horse stepped towards me I rode away. Over several sessions the horse was able to get closer and closer to the bike without showing any fear at all; indeed, by the end it was actively chasing me on the bike up and down the driveway. I have also used this technique to retrain a horse that was frightened of electric scooters. This was a much more fun process as it involved riding an electric scooter on my gravel driveway. Much less effort and a lot more speed.

In one of our university practical sessions we take a very large inflatable ball and, using approach conditioning, desensitize one of the university's mares. The ball moves in such an unnatural manner, and is so unlike anything most horses have ever seen, that initially they look at it with wide eyes and a great deal of mistrust. However, if done efficiently, they will quickly learn to step towards the ball with great confidence.

We then use a conditioned reinforcer and some high-value treats to teach our subject to touch the ball with her nose, and very quickly most horses will learn that a firm touch makes the ball roll away. Pretty soon they will be shoving the ball away with their noses, and what 20 minutes earlier had been a cause for great suspicion now has effectively become a vending machine for treats. No matter how many times I do this exercise I never tire of it. Despite knowing the science behind its success, to me it still feels just a little bit like magic. (I should also add that I never tire of seeing bread dough rise and will point out how magical it is to anyone within earshot. After spending their lifetimes listening to me expound the amazingness of dough my offspring simply roll their eyes and walk away. Perhaps I have desensitized them to the wonder that is dough rising.)

Systematic desensitization is when the horse is gradually and progressively introduced to the object that might otherwise frighten it. This is how most desensitization is done in training. It is common practice to limit the movement of the horse's legs when it is exposed to the scary stimulus because this limits the degree to which the flight response is demonstrated. However (and again, it's another big however), it is vitally important to introduce the stimulus at such a low threshold that the horse shows no fear throughout the process. If the handler ties the horse so that it can't get away or uses a harsh bit to control it and then bombards the horse with the frightening stimuli, that's just flooding with all its detrimental effects.

Systematic desensitization is a bit like the erosion method of desensitization. It occurs after time and a lot of repetition. If your horse lives in a paddock next to a railway line, she will eventually get used to trains. However, in the process she might also practise a lot of running away from trains. As we now know, there is no such thing as true extinction (that is, the behaviour always exists within the brain; it is simply suppressed), so systematic desensitization is a bit of a behavioural Russian roulette. You never know when the old fear response will rear its head.

Interestingly, horses are often surprisingly unbothered by the sight of planes in the sky. For an animal that will blindly bolt away from a blowing crisp packet it would seem likely that the sight of a huge, metal bird might be quite confronting. However, horses did not evolve in the time of the pterodactyl, therefore their evolution was untroubled by flying predators big enough to bother them.

Training for the farrier

I always find it useful to break a training task into as many small pieces as make it seem manageable. So, for example, when training a young horse for the farrier the task requires that the horse stands still, will pick up a designated hoof, will allow the hoof to be held, and is able to tolerate the sensation, smell and noise associated with being shod.

The first part of the behaviour involves teaching the young horse to stand still (or park; see page 240). Once she can park for a couple of minutes it is useful to practise standing still or parking in the place where she will eventually be shod. Then, when other horses are being shod, the young horse can practise parking nearby, moving closer and closer to the unfamiliar noise and smell of the other horses being shod. Don't rush this phase of the training — just like us, the young horse doesn't get less frightened of something by being forced into close proximity with it. She gets less frightened by *slowly and systematically* habituating to it.

Next, it's time to practise picking up the hooves, and I usually use a conditioned reinforcer when training this. The first phase is simply to pick up the hoof to reinforce that behaviour. If she kicks out when you try to handle her hind legs, begin by rubbing them all over with a long whip. Don't remove the whip until she stands quietly. Be generous with your reinforcements when she is still.

Once the hoof picking-up is established, you can start gradually adding time. Pick up the hoof and hold it for three seconds — reinforce that. Then pick up the hoof and hold it for five seconds — reinforce that. Remember the rules of shaping and don't ask for longer intervals until she is getting the previous interval correct. Also make sure that you use your conditioned reinforcer when the hoof is still in your hands (not on the ground) otherwise you're reinforcing a completely different behaviour. It's quite handy to grow an extra pair of hands for this phase but I've never managed it, so I usually just use a whistle as a conditioned reinforcer. If you have a friend who is happy to help out, that's even better.

Once you have at least a minute's duration trained for the hoof-holding behaviour, you can start adding some sensations by patting/rubbing the bottom of the hoof with your palm. Reward standing still by stopping the rubbing. Gradually add longer duration and more sensation. Borrow or buy a rasp and rub that across the bottom of the hoof. It's much easier at this stage to have a helper. If the horse pulls her foot out of your grasp, the handler should quickly step her backwards, then immediately repeat the pick-up/rubbing sequence.

If you're retraining an older horse that has become difficult for the farrier, the stepping backwards is a very important technique because it mitigates any expressions of the flight response. In my experience, when things go wrong in training it is often because small steps have been missed in the initial shaping of the behaviour. So, even with an older horse, it's useful to go through the whole training sequence from the very beginning. It's surprising how many times you will discover a big gap and while they often don't seem very significant to us, these gaps are quite often the instigator of the flight response.

As always, keep your training sessions short and try to get in as many reinforcements as is practical.

Overshadowing

As discussed earlier, overshadowing occurs because when two stimuli are presented at the same time, only the most salient will elicit a response. You can use any behaviour for overshadowing but the one that's most commonly used is forwards and backwards steps — just a couple in each direction.

This is another technique that requires two handlers. The horse is stepped forwards and backwards by one handler while the other introduces the scary thing — let's say clippers. I often find it useful to get the horse handler to give the forwards and backwards steps a mark out of ten for heaviness, where one is very light and ten is extremely heavy. In all our interactions with the horse, we want the signals we use for control to be between one and about two on this scale. Until the signals are light the handler is using more pressure than is comfortable for the horse just to manoeuvre his body, and that will create stress. It is very important in any overshadowing procedure that the horse begins with really light responses. If they're not light, the first step of the training process will be to improve them.

Initially, the clippers are introduced at a distance so great that the quality of the horse's responses remains unchanged — that is, they are no heavier than they were before the clippers appeared. As the handler with the clippers steps towards the horse, the horse handler will notice that the horse's responses become a little heavier or more delayed. This is the cue for the clippers to stay where they are until the forwards and backwards steps return to normal, at which point the clippers can come a little bit closer. And so on, and so on, until the clippers can be gently placed on the horse's shoulder.

This process should be repeated for all scary aspects of the clippers. For example, the clippers might be scary to look at, scary to feel, scary to hear and scary to smell. Batching all the scary aspects together makes them very aversive, so separate the scary aspects as much as possible. Present the clippers turned off in the beginning, so that the horse is thoroughly desensitized to the sight of them before you turn them on. Make sure the horse is thoroughly habituated to the sound and sight of them before, for example, letting them vibrate against his body.

Avoid fear!

If at any stage the horse shows a strong fear reaction, then what the horse has learned is that the clippers are scary. Because the horse can learn behaviours in a single trial (thanks to the HPA axis, or flight response), this is to be avoided at all costs. What is scary to the horse is totally subjective, just as what as scary to each individual person is totally subjective. I have seen so many riders get frustrated because their horse was frightened by something that they themselves didn't deem scary. But it is not the object that is important — it is the horse's reaction to it.

At home, during desensitization training, I often use a conditioned reinforcer to mark the desirable behaviour – which is usually park, or to stand still. With everything we do we are asking the horse to either habituate to a stimulus (such as the saddle, clippers, other horses in a warm-up arena, etc.) or sensitize to it (such as the rider's aids). So the horse must sort all new stimuli into either the habituate column or the sensitize one. By marking the behaviour of immobility with a conditioned reinforcer you make the sorting a little easier. As an example, if I was putting a light rug on a young horse for the first time, I would introduce the sight of the rug (at a distance way below threshold) and reinforce immobility, gradually getting closer and reinforcing every increment. I would reinforce the horse for standing still when the rug is gently placed against her shoulder, then laid (folded) across her back, and so on. In this way, the horse is starting what will be a lifelong behaviour calmly, there are no fear responses to cover over (because, remember, flight response behaviours are never eradicated, they are simply suppressed), and the rug now precedes and therefore predicts the onset of a food reward. By using reinforcers as part of the overshadowing process, counter conditioning and overshadowing are being used in sequence.

One of the positive aspects of utilizing overshadowing as a training technique is that it teaches riders to quickly assess their horse's mental state via the quality of the learned responses. It can be difficult, especially for novice riders, to gauge when their horse is overshadowed by the surroundings, for example at a show or in a new environment. A couple of minutes spent quietly stepping the horse forwards and backwards is a very good window into the horse's level of arousal. We use the step-back response in foundation training to gauge the horse's reaction to the weight of the rider for the first time – if the step back is heavy the horse needs more time to habituate.

Overshadowing can be used with purpose as a tool for desensitization, but it also often occurs inadvertently in training if the rider concurrently applies two aids. The traditional riding dictum is that the use of simultaneous leg and rein aids is part of the reason why horses, far more tactile and sensitive than we can ever dream of being, can still be habituated to the leg and rein aids to such a degree that harsh bits, nosebands and spurs are required to elicit forward and stop responses. Indeed, it is interesting to consider that as dressage horses progress through the levels, double bridles and spurs become compulsory equipment in competition.

Many equitation scientists believe that it is this fundamental flaw in dressage doctrine that is the root cause of many behaviour problems in the ridden horse, as the overshadowing leads to heavy and/or unreliable responses. Certainly, in my experience when retraining horses that have developed undesirable behaviours, there is always a problem with either the forwards or the stop response. In a study of over 100 horses, Dr Andrew McLean showed that there are very clear and predictable deficits associated with every problem behaviour. For example, horses that rear and also those that shy have a major deficit in their forwards response, whereas horses that buck and those that bolt have a major deficit in their stop response. However, it is very rare that these horses show deficits in only one response; they are almost always unreliable or heavy in their other responses, too.

It gets a bit technical here but bear with me. When a horse has a reliable forwards response not only does the forward response exist in the presence of the forward aid, but the forward response is absent in the absence of the aid. That is, the horse goes calmly forward when asked to but doesn't rush off randomly. The same is true for the stop response. This means that a horse with a clear and reliable forward response must also have a clear stop response. And vice versa. The two most important responses in the horse's repertoire are inextricably linked. So, while horses with poor forward responses are more likely to rear and shy, when tested those horses also have pretty poor stop responses, just slightly less poor than their forward response.

There is also a flow-on effect in the turn signals, too. It occurred to me a few years ago that horses that don't travel straight (that is, they don't stay on the rider's line without constantly being corrected) are the ones that most often don't have a good 'go' response. I suppose we can think of it like this: with our big prefrontal cortex we are good at seeing the big picture, at understanding the concept of 'forward'. The horse, with his big cerebellum, is more sensitive to the minutiae of movement. When horses travel straight their front legs protract (move forwards) and retract (move backwards) in a symmetrical way. The horse that travels crookedly, always falling one way or the other, is not only protracting and retracting but also randomly abducting (leg moves away from the body) and adducting (leg moves towards the body). Horses are excellent at forming habits and this randomness is detrimental to that process. So, a lack of clarity develops and this affects the rest of the horse's responses.

Crookedness is especially problematic for jumping horses, as an inability to travel straight not only makes the task of getting around a jumping course more difficult, it seems also to predispose the horse to being less careful with the front legs. I often paraphrase a well-known book and say that, in jumping horses, cleanliness is next to straightliness.

The flip side of habituation is sensitization, which is when the reaction increases after exposure to a stimulus. A good example of this is how horses can become sensitized to all wire after receiving a shock from an electric fence. A lot of fences are made from posts and white electric conducting tape, and most horses I know will not cross a strip of this tape on the ground, even if it isn't electrified. They have been sensitized to the sight of white conducting tape.

Sensitization is the reason why illegal and unethical (and downright cruel) 'jiggers' have been used in the racing industry by unscrupulous trainers. When horses are continuously hit with the whip during races they habituate to it and it eventually ceases to elicit a forward response. Seeking to make the whip more effective, some trainers have turned to a device known as a jigger, a whip that delivers a small but painful electric shock. This was foregrounded a few years ago when a very prominent Australian racehorse trainer was arrested after a police operation that involved placing hidden cameras around his property. We can only hope that the large fine he was given and his subsequent ban are a deterrent to other trainers.

Shaping

Shaping, or successive approximation as it is often called, is the process of gradually changing behaviours over time. A friend of mine says shaping reminds him of Michelangelo. Apparently the artist was once asked how he was able to create such amazing sculptures and he said that it was easy: you start with a big block of marble, a hammer and chisel, and you simply take away all the marble that you don't need. What is left is a beautiful sculpture. This is training. We don't train animals to do things they can't already do — we can never train a cat to fly or a horse to swim underwater — we simply reinforce the behaviours we want until that's what we get when we ask.

Behaviours don't emerge fully fledged. They take time to create and mould into their final form. The coaches of human gymnasts know this — after all, it would be quite cruel to expect a five-year-old to complete a triple somersault. Effective shaping is done by breaking down behaviours into manageable chunks and working on each part separately.

When you are shaping an animal to do a behaviour it's a little bit like going on a journey together. You don't always know what scenery you'll see on your journey, but you should know what your destination is. Sometimes I shape behaviours purely for the enjoyment of working with an animal. For example, one of my horses is a little bit sensitive about being brushed and I wanted to counter condition him. But I wanted to go one step further and get him to initiate the counter-conditioning process — in a way, for him to give me his consent for the brushing to begin.

So, initially I reinforced him for touching his nose to a big soft plastic cone. When he could reliably do that I moved the cone slightly to the side. Then we started a counter-conditioning sequence — one brush/treat, one brush/treat in a nice steady rhythm. When I guessed that he was anticipating the sequence continuing, I abruptly stopped it. He looked around for a way to turn me back into a treat-vending machine, spotted the cone and touched it with his nose and I brushed then treated. He quickly learned that to initiate the brush/treat sequence he needed to touch his nose to the cone. He now does this reliably and when he has had enough brushing he stops touching the cone.

This kind of training gives the animal agency over a potentially aversive stimulus. The animal learns to either initiate, maintain or terminate the experience. I've used similar protocols for girth tightening, rugging and clipping. They're very effective. I wish I could say that they were my idea but the first time I saw them they were being used for nail trimming with a reactive dog. The important thing to remember is that the cone touching initiates a brushing sequence, not the onset of something else that is potentially aversive. If you have a horse that dislikes being girthed and being brushed, you should use a separate behaviour to initiate each.

Don't rush

Sometimes when you're shaping, it can be tempting to rush ahead. The rule of thumb which is often used is: if the animal gets the answer right three times, raise the bar. If the animal hesitates or is slow, stay at the same criterion. If the animal gets it wrong, go back. Three times three sets of correct responses, a maximum number of three times per day (27 repetitions in total) is plenty.

Bob Bailey, one of the best-known animal trainers in the world, points out that you get the behaviour you reinforce, not necessarily the behaviour you want. This has to be one of the most important statements about animal training I've ever heard. If your learner is continually getting the answer wrong, it is to your own training that you must look. Is the reinforcer reinforcing enough? Is the timing of the reinforcer accurate? Is the shaping schedule appropriate? Have you failed to consolidate somewhere? In a training situation there should be no really aversive consequences if the horse trials the wrong behaviour. Someone once told me that a weed is just a plant growing in the wrong place. Mistakes in training are just behaviour in the wrong place at the wrong time. Remember, behaviours either wither or grow, depending on their consequences.

Differential reinforcement is a term used to describe the shaping of an already existing behaviour. It occurs when you withhold reinforcement for some forms of the behaviour while rewarding others. Differential reinforcement is often used to untrain already learned behaviours and can be used in a few different ways. Differential reinforcement of incompatible or alternative behaviour occurs when you train a behaviour that is incompatible with the behaviour you don't want. So, for example, if a horse nips when she is being girthed she can be trained to touch her nose to a target during saddling, because this behaviour is incompatible with girthing. Differential reinforcement of low rates of behaviour can be used for behaviours like pawing while tied up. If you reinforce the horse for standing still, the pawing will gradually reduce. (As an aside, pawing is a common behaviour for horses. It's hardwired. When hungry, wild horses will paw because the pawing either turns up edible roots below the ground or removes snow from the ground. Domestic horses paw when they have a problem they can't solve. You can think of it as a behaviour they do when they are trapped between their instincts and their current situation. Punishing it is ineffective and only serves to create more anxiety.)

During both horse and elephant training clinics, we sometimes play a neat game called PORTL to help teach some of the complexities of shaping. Participants are paired, one takes the role of the animal (or more politically correctly, the learner) and one is the trainer. The trainer is given a clicker (to use as a conditioned reinforcer) and a box of small objects. The box I use has, amongst other things, dice, a toy car, a short ruler, a plastic rhino and some different coloured blocks and buttons. After an explanation of the various shaping tools, the trainer (without the learner seeing) is shown a card on which is written a technique and, using the small objects and the clicker as a reinforcer, must use that technique on the learner. The techniques are:

» Differential reinforcement: you get more of what you reinforce. The trainer should only reinforce certain behaviours; for example touch the red button, or behaviours in a certain context, such as only move the car from left to right, not right to left.

» Extinction: behaviour that's no longer reinforced will decrease in frequency. The trainer reinforces a simple behaviour such as put the rhino on top of the toy car and then, once established, stop reinforcing that behaviour. This can be extremely frustrating for the learner and can sometimes be accompanied by an extinction burst, which is a significant increase in the behaviour before it diminishes. (When I played this game with my hard-working, overachieving partner his extinction burst was both complex and determined!)

- Reset: the trainer returns the object to its starting point. For example, the learner picks up the car and moves it, then resets it to where it started. This has the effect of making the behaviour very specific to the context in which it occurred.
- Targeting: the learner moves an object to another object. As an example, the trainer reinforces the learner for pushing the car from left to right, then puts a block in the car's path and reinforces the seemingly inadvertent driving of the car to the block. The trainer can gradually, using other objects to navigate around, train the learner to push the car through different patterns such as circles and figure eights. If the objects are gradually removed, the learner will eventually complete the same figures.
- Transferring actions: some actions are more likely to occur with certain objects. For example, the learner is much more likely to drive a car than roll a dice. By training one action, you can transfer it to another object.

- Changing the criteria for reinforcement: if you want to increase the frequency of a behaviour, withholding reinforcement for an already established behaviour can be an effective method. For example, if you establish a behaviour of touching the car then withhold reinforcement for that behaviour, the learner will often try touching the car again.
- Building behaviour chains: when teaching more complex behaviours it's useful to train them one piece at a time. Train each piece of the chain separately until fluent, then add them together. For example, the task might be to stack three blocks, with red on top, green in the middle, and yellow on the bottom. The learner is reinforced for stacking the red on the green. The trainer removes the red. The learner is reinforced for stacking the green on the yellow. When fluent, the trainer doesn't reinforce the learner for stacking the green on the yellow but adds the red block. When the learner stacks the red onto the green on yellow stack, they are reinforced. After a few repetitions all three blocks can be presented together.

The principles of shaping

There are a few rules that most good trainers adhere to when shaping:

- » Be prepared!
- » Break down each behaviour into its smallest components.
- » Train one criterion at a time.
- » Relax criteria when something changes.
- » If it's not working it's not the learner's fault — change something.
- » Maintain a high rate of reinforcement.
- » Revise if necessary.
- » Keep your attention on the learner.
- » Stay ahead of your learner . . . know what the next step might look like.
- » Quit while you're ahead.

Welfare

Animal welfare has always been a subjective topic. Our thousands of years of coexistence with the horse and a tendency towards anthropomorphism have caused some less-than-ideal welfare assumptions to embed themselves in popular opinion. To me, the most obvious one is the common assumption that horses appreciate being stabled throughout the night, when nothing in the horse's 55-million-year evolution suggests this is the case. As we have already discussed, the horse is largely crepuscular, not diurnal, so doesn't go to bed in the evening and sleep till morning. We like the idea of going to bed at night, but the horse is naturally most active at dawn and dusk, so the stable is a place of confinement, not sleep. Also, wild horses walk somewhere from 25 kilometres (15½ mi) up to 80 kilometres (50 mi) per day, which suggests that their mental state and much of their physiology probably works best when they are moving. Some horses may appear keen to enter a stable but that is because they are usually fed as soon as they enter (or at least have a hay net). If the stable door was left open, they would soon leave once the food was finished.

As an aside, just as in the developed world we are becoming increasingly overweight and prone to the lifestyle diseases that accompany too much food and not enough physical activity, so too are the animals that share our world having the quality of their lives impacted by the same factors. It's important that we prioritize good (i.e. not excessive and as minimally processed as possible) nutrition and an adequate amount of physical activity so that our animals can live happily and as full of health and vitality as possible.

The Five Freedoms model

It was because of the subjective nature of welfare assessment that the Five Freedoms model of animal welfare was devised as an objective tool to assess and improve the welfare of the animals that live alongside us.

The Five Freedoms model was first used in 1965 and, in the following three decades it became a widely used tool for assessing welfare. The five freedoms are:

1. freedom from hunger and thirst
2. freedom from discomfort
3. freedom from pain, injury and disease
4. freedom to express normal behaviour
5. freedom from pain and distress.

However, there are limitations to this model. If we were to apply the Five Freedoms to humans we would see that, within the framework of the model, human prisoners in most Western jails would be deemed to have adequate (even good) welfare because they are well fed, relatively free from discomfort, able to seek medical care and about as able to express natural (human) behaviours as most domestic animals. And this demonstrates well the limitations of the Five Freedoms as a way of assessing welfare, because we now understand that it takes more than just an absence of detrimental elements to ensure that an animal's life is fulfilling.

Researchers Professor David Mellor and Dr Cam Reid set out to produce a new welfare model that reflects this understanding, and in 1994 they proposed their new model of animal welfare, now known as the Five Domains. This model has largely taken over from the Five Freedoms. The greatest difference between the two models is that the Five Domains recognizes that animals have emotional needs and that the ability to fulfil these needs is the difference between a life and a life worth living.

In 2020 the Five Domains model was updated and now, thanks to the input of Dr Andrew McLean, recognizes the importance of an animal's interactions with humans. It also shows how an animal's mental state (the fifth domain) is ultimately a product of the sum and interaction of the other four physiological and behavioural domains.

The Five Domains are:

1. Nutrition. When trying to achieve optimal welfare it is not enough for an animal to have sufficient calories to survive. Food should be varied and reflect the animal's evolved dietary needs. Overeating is not optimal either.

2. Living environment. Animals have unique living requirements and these should be taken into consideration when designing living quarters. Factors such as space, light and ventilation should be taken into consideration.
3. Health and fitness. The model shows that while an undernourished, overworked animal has poor welfare, so too does an obese, largely sedentary one. Injury and disease have a negative impact on welfare.
4. Behavioural interactions. This domain is divided into three parts: interactions with the environment; interactions with other animals; and interactions with humans. This domain deals with the quality of the animal's environment, the animal's ability to interact naturally with other animals and the quality of the care the animal receives from humans.
5. Mental state. This domain is a direct result of the interaction of the previous four domains and reflects the ability of the previous four to adequately satisfy the animal's evolved needs.

When we view welfare through the lens of the Five Domains model it's easy to see how the horse's training can significantly impact its welfare. Because we understand that the horse's brain is different to ours, we can see that so-called 'naughty' horses are not content. They are usually just confused and almost certainly in the grip of the flight response.

The two pillars of training welfare

Many scientific studies have shown that there are two important components when trying to reduce stress in both animals and humans: predictability and controllability. I like to think of them as the two pillars of training welfare. When we see them in the context of the Five Domains, we can see that they are at the heart of the fourth domain, behavioural interactions.

As controllability and predictability are so important to the horse's mental wellbeing, it's really worthwhile prioritizing them whenever we can. Fortuitously, they are part of the outcome of good training. I'll explain . . .

When the pressure cues we use to lead and ride the horse adhere to the rules of negative reinforcement, this gives the horse a degree of controllability over the pressure that is used because the cues start extremely light and gradually increase over a predictable timeframe. Horses are pressure avoidant, so being able to remove pressure cues is very important for their mental wellbeing.

When those pressure cues are consistent and well established the horse learns, via classical conditioning, to predict their onset, in the same way that Clever Hans was able to predict that the very subtle change in von Osten's posture preceded and therefore predicted the food reward. Thus the combination of negative reinforcement and classical conditioning, when applied well, gives the horse both controllability and predictability.

These same rules apply to all domestic animals: good, consistent training is one way we can ensure the welfare of our animal companions is as optimal as possible.

ARKADY

2125

Grandfather stacks empty wine bottles like others might stack kindling. When the wind blows right it plays them like a flute and Arkady remembers his mother, who used to sing. Grandfather remembers the music too, which is why Arkady's receiver is a tangle of coloured wires and shards of broken plastic in a small box under his bed.

He misses the music. At night he hears the wild dogs on the hill and wishes he could muffle their barking with songs. But the old man's arm is strong despite the drink, the receiver is in pieces and on the sooted kitchen wall there is a white thumbnail of missing plaster.

Memories ride Grandfather as though one day his knees will buckle under the weight of them. On a day when the horizon is lost to the smoke of burning stubble fields, he nails the east-facing windows of the house shut. Mismatched boards across the glass, his mouth full of nails. Afterwards, the house closes its eyes to the scorched paddocks and to the small garden where Arkady's mother used to sing. In the early morning, hard squints of sunlight and shade bar the floor black and the brilliant orange of a nuclear sunrise.

In the one-roomed school Arkady learns that it hasn't always been this way. He learns that before the war the sun would set and rise without fanfare, and that the wilderness had once been farms and suburbs. That there had been jobs and shops and hospitals. That, in their town, people had out-numbered graves. But that was before. Now, between the sunrise and Grandfather's house is the place where nobody lives, just the wild dogs they say have been made as big as bears by radiation. Arkady doesn't know why radiation has made dogs big but people small and then smaller still, until you could see their ribs through their clothes when they cough. And then gone.

On Sundays, Arkady goes with his grandfather to the small stone church, shoulder to shoulder with the rest of the town, the smell of picked tobacco and sweated-in wool. The priest wears work boots beneath his robes and his fingers are edged with half-moons of old sump oil but Arkady likes the songs, the feel of singing in his chest and the solid bodies beside his on the hard wooden pew. Sometimes, if the night has been long, Grandfather's eyes will close and his head will drop onto his chest. He loves the old man most then, quiet, and his big knuckled hands aground in his lap.

~

Arkady was shit scared and fourteen the first time he went into the exclusion zone. Rust had seized the boom gates and from a distance the three-bladed fan looked like a faded Christmas angel. He slipped beneath the gate, onto a road that was pocked with clumps of grass and the bulge of tree roots. After walking for ten minutes he could no longer see the town and after 20 minutes could no longer hear the wind farm or the road, just the hush of insects and a birdsong unfamiliar to him. He saw an eagle and, on an old bridge warped by the seasons, he lay on his belly and watched the copper flit of bream in the river below.

Later, back in the town, he wondered if people could see the change on him, like a mark or a brand. He woke at night and remembered the shadows of small birds quick across the ground and the smell of the wind. He took the long road home from school so he could look past the gate and down the track that led into the patchy forest. And the next time he was able, he slipped back into the exclusion zone again.

The clouds were low that day and heavy with rain. He smelled the fox before he saw it. Like the smell of an old fur collar, musty and damp at the back of his throat. He was close enough to see the dark-rimmed ears and the russet taper of its legs. It crossed the broken road ahead of him, pausing to glance in his direction before disappearing into the long grass. He paused for a moment and then followed.

He walked and walked, raising small birds from the undergrowth, his trousers wet with dew. An old dairy filled with empty troughs and rat scurry leaned into a hill, open to the sky and its walls aslant. Behind it an orchard. He wandered down the rows where, amongst the leaves, unripe plums clustered small as berries and a lemon tree creaked with unpicked fruit.

Behind the orchard was a house, the front door rusting off its hinges. Arkady moved slowly through rooms papery with dust. In places the ceiling had fallen in and above he could see rafters bowed like rib bones. To a kitchen cabinet fretted with webs was pinned a faded picture of three girls running and playing. Though watermarked and specked with mould he could see that the sun was shining. He took it down and smoothed the picture flat; written on the back was the number 2098, the year before the war began. He counted on his fingers. In 2098 his mother would have been ten, about the same age as the girls running and playing in the photo.

Arkady could no longer remember his mother's smile. Five days after they buried her Grandfather had built a small pyre of her things — a handful of books, photos and the soft shirts that smelled like home. He was only three and had cried to see all the pretty colours burning. He looked at the photo in his hand. Maybe it was her. Maybe it was his mother in the old photo, running and playing on a day long ago when it seemed like the sun would shine forever.

He smiled and carefully slipped the brittle paper into his pocket.

~

Grandfather tells him that when the minerals ran out in the last decade of the 21st century a lot of people left for places where the rain still fell. By then the forests were long gone and the wheatfields that had once fed the whole country were glittery with salt, like fields of broken glass.

'We were happy when they built the reactor,' Grandfather says. 'Jobs for us who knew nothing but ripping up the ground. And enough power to make good water from the sea.'

He lights a thinly rolled cigarette with the glowing end of another and blows smoke from the side of his mouth. 'It seems impossible now that we could have been that bloody stupid.'

Grandfather smokes in silence for a while. 'Turns out you don't need to build bombs when there are reactors loaded with uranium – you just hack the control system.' Then he fans out his fingers and draws a circle through the smoke with his palms. 'Boom, it's all over.'

~

The day he first saw the horses, Arkady was almost seventeen and almost two days walk from home. He had camped overnight in a rickety hayshed, unrolling his sleeping bag on a pile of old chaff bags. In the deepening twilight he had eaten beans from a jar, so quietly that the sound of his breath and the shir of insects seemed loud. The next morning was cold enough to mist his breath. He sat in the doorway eating his last chunk of bread when he saw something moving at the edge of the paddock.

The small herd moved out from the cover of the trees, flinchy and short stepping. They were all the browns of polished timber. He could see their nostrils test the wind and the shine of their wide-held eyes. They were nubbled with muscle, short legged and barrelly. Arkady held his breath, the dry bread forgotten in his mouth, and felt the joy of them like a balloon rising, warm, inside his chest.

The first into the open was a mare and then the stallion, his neck heavy-crested. Behind them three more mares, one with a spindle-legged foal at foot, and behind them three yearlings with tufty foal coats half-grown out. The lead mare stopped and stared into the tree line at the barn where Arkady huddled inside his jacket, so still he could feel the pulse of his blood in his ears. Through the trees and across the field of hip-high grass he held her gaze.

Moments passed. And then she dropped her head and began to graze. Arkady hugged his knees. He saw that the mare's belly was taut behind her ribs and wondered if she was pregnant. He let out his breath bit by bit and watched the horses in the field. In places the grass rose to their chests, and they floated through it like boats, their backs broad. The early sun was on their coats like honey and Arkady wished he could walk through the grass with them, run his palms along the curve and swell of their bodies, through the long tangles of their manes. They would smell, he thought, like fields of undulating grass, spring wind and endless open sky. He wished more than anything that he could close his eyes, press his face into their necks and breathe in the shine and the warmth of them.

When he stretched the ache out of his legs the big mare lifted her head, a tuft of grass dangling, forgotten, from her lips. She watched him for a moment then gave a small shake of her mane and settled back to grazing, occasionally flicking a pointed ear in his direction. By the time the sun was over the treetops he could yawn or reach for the heel of stale bread without startling her.

And then, when the sun was warmest overhead, the horses turned and mingled back into the scrub. He looked away for a moment and they were gone, the trees making shadows of their bodies. He waited but the paddock seemed barren without them and he was a long way from home.

~

Grandfather keeps a blackened pan of soup on the range, each night adding potatoes or carrots from the garden. When there is money in his pocket he throws the old bones to the neighbour's pig and brings new ones, wrapped in newspaper, home from the market. There are times when the soup is just salt and greens but the week after Arkady saw the horses, when he was hollow with long nights and growing, the soup was ham hock and dried peas and bread thick-sliced for dipping.

They ate for a while in silence till Grandfather tapped his spoon against his plate.

'The soup will not grow legs and walk away.' He nodded. 'Slow down or you'll get the bloat.'

Arkady smiled. 'I'm not one of your sheep.'

Grandfather blew out through loose lips. 'So you say. But let's not test the theory, okay?'

'Sorry. But it's so good.'

'You flatter my cooking to excuse your table manners?'

'Well, no, it's good. But also, yes.'

Grandfather grunted. 'Honesty has always been your weakest trait.'

Arkady ate slowly until his belly was full.

'In the exclusion zone,' he said, the last of his bread still half chewed in his mouth, 'I saw horses. Mostly brown ones with dark-coloured manes. Some a darker brown, though.'

The old man looked at him across the table, unblinking.

'First swallow, then talk.'

Arkady swallowed and wiped the back of his hand across his mouth.

'They looked strong. Beautiful.'

Grandfather cleared his throat.

'Horses?'

'Yes,' and he counted on his fingers. 'Nine of them.'

Grandfather folded his arms across his chest.

Arkady ate for a while in silence. 'Before the war,' he said, 'they used to ride them, right?'

His grandfather blew smoke from the side of his mouth. 'I never did. But my grandfather, yes.'

'I wonder what it was like. Did he ever say?'

'No, he didn't,' and Grandfather shook his head. 'Don't waste your thoughts on it. That was then and this is now.'

'But don't you think it would be the most incredible thing?'

His grandfather stared hard at him, frowning.

'What I think is that if the Flatlanders caught you sneaking around they might shoot first and ask questions later. They might wonder who would miss a boy allowed to run wild where no one is supposed to go?'

~

The next day after school Arkady went on his bike to the small library in the next town. Empty paddocks passed him, and when he arrived he rubbed one worn boot against the other to move the mud that had dried on the edge of each sole. The librarian looked up as he entered the room, her desk a square of paraffin light, and he nodded and hurried to the nearest shelf.

He walked along the rows of books, his fingers along the ruck of spines like he was running his hands down his own ribcage. He breathed in the smell. A kind of closeness, earthy, a fire-warming leather. He had a sudden memory of his mother reading, pages turning, his head pillowed against her belly. The words a blanket. And he, the kind of warm that forgets there is cold.

He remembered the feel of her skirt, the well-washed cotton against his face, and was trying to remember the colour when there was a polite cough, the librarian was next to him and his mother was gone. He felt for a moment like he'd been sitting too close to the fire, cheeks hot and throat tight. He needed to blink. She smiled at him and was old, her skin like a map of rivers. Each knuckle a walnut of bone and her wrists tiny. And him with his jumper all unravelled at the edges and his hands flapping big like tethered ducks.

'Can I help you?' she said and laid her hand lightly on the knit of his sleeve. He started to shake his head but felt the bird weight of her fingers and her smile and, then, he nodded.

'I was hoping to learn something,' he said quickly. 'About horses.'

She looked up at him and then nodded. 'Please. Follow me.'

In the next aisle she bent and pulled a large book from the shelf, took it back to her desk and opened it. She stepped aside and he could see that it was old, the corners thumbed to the thinness of skin.

She looked at him and said carefully, 'There haven't been horses around here for 50 years — but they say,' her voice reedy, 'that the last dronage showed some small herds. Can you imagine? Even before the war there were not many left. And after it, of course, even fewer.'

She waved her hand at her chair so that he would sit.

'So, they are survivors. Just like us.'

She patted his arm with fingers slender as bone. 'But I will leave you to read. If you need anything I'll be here.'

Arkady finished reading and closed the book. The librarian met him at the door.

'Thank you,' he said.

'The horses in the forest, you have seen them?' she asked and her eyes were bright.

He paused and looked around at the empty room.

'I won't tell,' she said and touched her lips with a forefinger.

'Yes,' he said. 'A stallion, some mares and some foals. I watched them grazing. They're beautiful. Strong, just like the pictures.' Arkady paused and the old woman nodded for more.

'There was one, the biggest mare. She was the boss, you could see. She watched me. If I moved she was careful. And then she got less worried. Like she realized I wouldn't hurt them. And there was one new foal and I think maybe three of last year's foals, half grown. And the big mare might be pregnant and maybe two of the other mares as well.'

'Such good news,' she said, smiling.

She watched him for a moment, her head tipped like a bird's.

'I know you,' she said.

'Sorry? What do you mean?'

'You are so much like your mother.'

'You knew her?'

'She was my friend.'

He shook his head sadly. 'I can't remember her and Grandfather won't.'

She reached out and touched his sleeve. 'Your mother was worth the pain of remembering.'

Arkady shrugged. 'There's nothing left now, anyway.'

'But there is,' she said softly and pressed two fingers to the middle of her chest. 'She is here. I can tell you. The books she loved, her favourite flowers. The songs she would sing to you.'

Arkady nodded, unsure of his voice.

She looked at the old clock on the wall. 'But you should go now, the roads aren't safe in the dark,' she said. 'Come back soon though. We have so much to talk about.'

He nodded at her and turned for the door.

She smiled. 'Go safely, Arkady.'

~

The next time Arkady goes into the exclusion zone the round plumpness of spring is gone. Grass grains fat with sap have hardened into dry sheaves and the stalks are stiff beneath his feet. He walks quietly along the slight, winding tracks of animals, his boots so worn at the sole he can feel tree roots where they break the ground.

The day is warm and he makes his way along an old road. Trees have pushed their way through the crumbly bitumen, and in the gaps they have made, grasses and small shrubs flourish. A pair of magpies follows him for the insects that fly up at his feet and out of the corner of his eye he sees a tapered tail disappear into the long grass beside the road.

He camps near the field where he had seen the horses, hoping to see them again. The evening, when it comes, is cool so he huddles in his sleeping bag and eats a meal of bread and hard cheese. Afterwards, tired, he lies and watches the moon rise and the tree shadows shortening. Just before he falls asleep he sees an owl in flight, its great wings white against the sky, as silent as ash falling.

They come the next morning, as beautiful as he remembered. The big mare in the lead and the others jostling behind her, grass to their knees. There is a new foal nimbling beside its mother and the big mare is heavy and slower than before. While the others graze she dozes in the sun, first resting one hind leg, then the other. She watches him carefully when he moves and he can see, from a distance, her nostrils flair for his scent.

By late morning, if he is careful and moves slowly, he can stand up or drink from his water bottle without her taking fright. And just like before, when the sun reaches its full height they are gone, leaving the open field empty and him with nothing better to do than start the long walk home.

That summer the sky is a hot blue bowl. No rain for months, the dust under his feet thick like flour and his walk to cut branches for their ribby sheep getting longer and longer each day. The leaves on the fruit trees curl inwards away from the sun and their small house is dense with heat.

When Grandfather raps his knuckles on the side of their water tank he has to bend to his knees before it stops clanking hollowly.

'Soon we will have to bath in the dirt like chickens,' he says, shaking his head. 'And make our morning coffee out of wine.'

~

Arkady is so often in the exclusion zone that summer that the herd no longer startles at his approach. One day the big mare is missing and he spends the night restless and anxious, scared that something has happened to her. But the next day she returns with a dark, leggy colt at her side and he lies on his stomach in the dried grass and watches them, side by side and together so tender he thinks he has never in his life seen anything as perfect.

As the summer draws on the herd has to travel further each day for water and he begins to see the shadows of ribs on the yearlings. In places the river has dried to small pools of green water, like glass beads strung on a winding riverbed of darkly dried mud. He no longer watches them disappear into the forest but follows them through the trees, along the winding paths they have made through the undergrowth. When they stop to rest he lies down nearby and sometimes the older foals, bold and curious, get so close that he can almost reach out and touch them.

One morning he waits for the herd by the field where they often spend the morning. The sun is higher when they finally arrive and they are quick and anxious, snatching mouthfuls of the dry grass and listening with their heads up. He counts and realizes with a sudden shrinking of his vision that there is no sign of the big mare and her colt.

Arkady watches the herd, his heart squinting in his chest. The morning is still and already hot and in the thin air he hears, faintly, the sound of a horse neighing, frantic. He runs across the field, scattering the rest of the herd, and stops to listen, then changes direction, threading his way through the trees.

He sees her by a water hole. She is running along a small stretch of riverbed and her hooves have churned the mud to paste, dark streaks all the way up to her belly. She is foamed with sweat and he can smell her panic, her neighing rasping breaths. Arkady, running, feels his own breath hot in his lungs and he follows her gaze until he sees her foal, her beautiful foal, sunk and drowning in a wallow of deep mud at the edge of the water.

She swerves around him without taking her eyes from her foal. Arkady can see that the little colt is almost exhausted, his neck bowed and the velvet of his nostrils sinking into the mud. For a moment he is undecided, the mud is deep and he is scared they might both sink — but then without thinking he starts pulling off his boots and shirt. He sucks a deep breath and takes into his lungs the smell of soil and stagnant water. For a moment he sees everything as though it is painted, the trees etched against the sky, too blue, leaves gilded by the early light. And the song of the magpies and the wind through the reeds is sweet and the sun on his back like a caress.

Into the mud at the edge of the pool and he begins sinking. For a moment he almost loses his courage, almost backs out of the water but the little colt's eyes are glassy and he hears the sawing breath of the mare on the bank. There are patches of firmer ground beneath his feet like stepping stones and he slides each foot through the mud, his toes arched to feel. The foal struggles weakly as he gets closer but from somewhere deep inside him come words and a melody and the memory of a hand, gentle on his cheek. A lullaby, and he sings it softly. *Day is done, gone the sun, from the lake, from the hills, from the sky*. Over and over, edging slowly closer.

When he is able, he burrows his arms through the mud and pulls the foal to his body. It is stronger than he thought, small hooves kicking sharp against his shins. Then, as he starts to back out of the wallow, his foot slips into soft ground. He is sinking, holding the foal. Thick mud over his shoulders, the weight of the colt pushing him down. He fights it hard, the sound of his own heartbeat in his ears and his breath so ragged he tastes metal in his mouth.

Until at last beneath his foot is solid ground and he would smile if he could have but his mouth is too wide open for air. He staggers onto dry ground and they stumble over, the foal clasped to his chest, its small weight pinning him. The big mare rushes towards them, he sees the sharp hardness of her hooves cleave the ground and for a moment he is frightened, but she stops and drops her head to her foal, whickering and nuzzling.

After a few minutes he helps the colt stagger to its feet. On tottery legs it begins to nurse and he squats beside the mare and foal, his body aching and glazed with mud like porcelain.

The mare turns to him. Slowly, he reaches his hand out towards her. She is wide eyed and cautious but doesn't move away, her nostrils gathering him in, his hand between them.

Slowly, she bends her head towards him. Then, for a moment he feels it, feels the warm touch of her breath against the backs of his fingers. And, as though he is dreaming, he sees a cascade of other moments reflected in the depths of her eye. An ancient land dusted with the last of the season's snow, a man in fur on a big-bodied mare, fleet and dreaming of the gods. A long line of ponies and people, a journey to a new land. A desperate siege, a horse made from wood. A carriage horse lipping bread from an old man's hands. Heavy horses straining in the harness and plough tines carving lines into soil. Hoofbeats and bullets, the sounds of dying men. Horses galloping and the sound of cheering. A young girl with her arms around the neck of a dark-bay horse. A woman saying goodbye.

The blood in him drums his chest like hoofbeats, hot and sharp and nestled in the place where where joy lives. And he knows with a sudden rush of certainty that he is now a tiny part of a story that began before time. A story of need and courage, and of love. But most of all, a story that isn't yet over. The story of the horse.

EPILOGUE

What does the future look like for the horse? How does a prehistoric brain and a body adapted for endless plains cope with an increasingly crowded and mechanized world? And what about breeding? Can we just keep on breeding horses for every task and with every trait that we desire — racehorses that run faster, dressage horses with more and more extreme movement, show horses with prettier arrangements of spots? What happens to these animals when they're no longer fast enough or pretty enough for the task for which they were bred?

Just because we can now breed chickens for the table that are fully mature in under six weeks, breed dogs so small that they can fit in a pocket, and clone entire teams of polo ponies, is it always ethical to do so? Can we be optimistic that the animals we produce will have the opportunity to live fulfilling lives? One thing that is certain is that we don't really know everything there is to know about genes and what might happen when we select exclusively for one trait above all else.

The silver fox

Russian biologist Dmitry Belyaev, working with silver foxes in the Russian fur industry wondered what would happen if he selected foxes based purely on temperament. The experiment began in 1959 and, although Dmitry died in 1985, it continues to this day under the watchful eye of Lyudmila Trut.

Dmitry was interested in the changes that occurred in wild species when they were domesticated. He chose 130 wild silver foxes from a fur-breeding farm in Estonia, and from the age of one month tested the foxes for tameness. One of Dmitry's students would offer food to a baby fox and attempt to pat it at the same time. In addition, they also watched to see whether the foxes preferred the company of other foxes or humans. When the foxes reached sexual maturity at seven to eight months of age, they were tested again and given an overall score for tameness. Only those foxes that were the least fearful and least aggressive were chosen for breeding; this worked out to less than 20 per cent of the population.

After 40 generations of selective breeding, the eventual result is a group of friendly, domesticated foxes in which 75 per cent of each litter will pass the test for tameness. But the most fascinating aspect of this experiment is that these domesticated foxes, which have been bred on the basis of a single selection criteria, now display distinct physiological and anatomical characteristics that are not found in the original 130 animals. This is extraordinary, because the criterion used to determine whether an individual fox would be allowed to breed was simply how they reacted to humans.

The domesticated foxes are not only tame, they whimper to attract attention and lick their carers. They wag their tails when they are happy or excited. They are a great deal less fearful than their ancestors and more eager to explore new situations. More interestingly, though, they display physiological changes that seem unrelated to their tameness. Many of them have floppy ears, short or curly tails, longer reproductive seasons, broken coat colours (black and white instead of silver) and changes in the shapes of their jaws and teeth. The domesticated foxes have tails that are often three to six vertebrae shorter, and they also have shorter snouts.

Researchers now have a fully sequenced fox genome for both the wild and tame silver foxes, showing 103 genomic regions that differ between the two groups. One of the most significant is that the tame foxes have a version of a gene called SorCS1 that does not appear in the wild foxes. In humans this gene is associated with Alzheimer's disease and autism, while in mice it is involved with synapse formation and neuron signalling. Other genetic differences between the domestic and wild fox genome are associated with the fight or flight response (the HPA axis). The domestic foxes have a smaller reaction to stress than their wild counterparts and this reaction is not simply a function of the environment in which they have been raised, but clearly has a genetic component, too.

What does this mean for us? The silver fox experiment tells us that we simply do not know everything there is to know about what happens when we base selection on very limited criteria. If we breed purely for jumping potential, is it possible that other, less desirable, traits may emerge? If we breed only for speed, are we also breeding horses that will stay sound enough to live normal, healthy lives when their racing days are over? To be good and honourable custodians of the horse we must be careful what we wish for in terms of genes. We must never let our quest for perfection or our subjective notions of beauty blind us to common sense and an understanding of what is both good for the individual and the future of the species as a whole.

~

As a child I decided that Christianity wasn't for me because there was no mention in the Bible of horses or dogs going to heaven. And I believed then, as I believe now, that a world without animals is not the sort of world I want to inhabit.

I wouldn't want to spend time in a place that only allowed humans because, in my opinion, some of the finest souls to walk this earth have done it on hooves and paws.

I was recently speaking with a wise friend of mine about ageing and he said, 'I've probably only got another horse left in my lifetime.' I've thought a lot about that and I have decided that for those of us who love them, there's probably no better measure of our own existence than the number of horses whose lives we have shared. For thousands of years horses have lived amongst us, their years spinning out like ours, but in fast-forward. We watch them grow from wobbly-legged foals into magnificent adults and finally into fragile old age. And what their much shorter lives teach us is that nothing is forever, no matter how much we wish it could be.

When you say goodbye to a much-loved horse a piece of you goes with them. You might look for that part of yourself in the sand wallow where they used to doze or in the cool jade stand of kikuyu underneath the plane tree. But that part of you has gone and you'll always feel that missing, even when the next horse comes along and takes its place in the hill paddock behind the house.

The last time I said goodbye to a horse I cradled his beautiful, bay head against my chest and whispered the only two words that seemed appropriate.

Thank you.

Thank you for allowing me to be a part of something far bigger than myself. Thank you for the joy that you have given. Thank you for the sense of awe that you inspired.

I know without a doubt that someday, when he goes to that place where I cannot yet follow, the horse I love now will take a part of my heart with him. But that is a pittance to pay considering what I have received in return.

I think that it is perhaps humanity's most redeeming feature that we unconditionally love our animals, knowing from the outset that one day they'll leave us broken-hearted. By loving the horse we become part of a story that is thousands of years old. A rich tapestry of mutual need that has been added to by countless generations. The past is indelible, but our own small part of the story can help shape the future and how we keep and train the horse today has enormous significance for generations still to come. Despite what the bill of sale or the registration papers state, we never truly own the horse. What we own is the right to hold the future of his species in trust for generations still to come, so that they too may feel the same joy and love and sense of awe that we do.

REFERENCES

This book has been a labour of both love and years. An extensive and complete reference list would consume dozens of pages so I have included here the key texts that were used or ones that particularly interest me.

I have used both reference books and academic articles in the compilation of this book and I am including a list of the most important ones. Luckily for interested readers it is easy now to search the internet for peer-reviewed information. I remember spending hours and hours in the stacks of my university's library searching out journal articles when I was doing my PhD. Funnily enough I remember those times with great fondness, even though I am now very grateful to have all the knowledge of the world at my fingertips in my home office.

Bachmann, I., Audige, L. and Stauffacher, M. (2003), 'Risk factors associated with disorders of crib-biting, weaving and box walking in Swiss horses', *Equine Veterinary Journal*.

Baer, K., Potter, G., Friend, T. and Beaver, B. (1994), 'Observation effects on learning in horses', *Applied Animal Ethology.*

Fiske, J. and Potter, G. (1979), 'Discrimination reversal learning in yearling horses', *Journal of Animal Science.*

Goodwin, D. (2007), 'Equine learning behaviour: What we know, what we don't and future research priorities', *Behavioural Processes.*

Henshall, C. and McGreevy, P. (2014), 'The role of ethology in round pen horse training: A review', *Applied Animal Behaviour Science.*

Jones, B. and McGreevy, P. (2010), 'Ethical equitation: Applying a cost benefit approach', *Journal of Veterinary Behaviour.*

Low, P. et al. (2012), 'The Cambridge Declaration on Consciousness. Proceedings of the Francis Crick Memorial Conference', Churchill College, Cambridge University, pp. 1–2.

McDonnell, S. and Haviland, J. (1995), 'Agonistic ethogram of the equid bachelor band', *Applied Animal Behaviour Science.*

McGreevy, P. (2007), 'The advent of equitation science', *The Veterinary Journal.*

McGreevy, P. and McLean, A. (2007), 'The role of learning theory and ethology in equitation', *Journal of Veterinary Behaviour.*

McGreevy, P. and McLean, A. (2009), 'Punishment in horse training and the concept of ethical equitation', *Journal of Veterinary Behaviour.*

McLean, A. (2013), 'Training the ridden animal: An ancient hall of mirrors', *The Veterinary Journal.*

McLean, A. and Christensen, J. (2017), 'The application of learning theory in horse training', *Applied Animal Behaviour Science.*

Nicol, C. (1996), 'Farm animal cognition', *Journal of Animal Science.*

Rollin, B. (2000), 'Equine welfare and emerging social ethics', *Journal of the American Veterinary Association.*

Scofield, R. and Randle, H. (2013), 'Preliminary comparison of behaviours exhibited by horses ridden in bitted and bitless bridles', *Journal of Veterinary Behaviour.*

Seligman, M. and Maier, S. (1967), 'Failure to escape traumatic shock', *Journal of Experimental Psychology.*

Books

For the chapters on the evolution and history of the horse I was most grateful to Pita Kelekna's excellent book *The Horse in Human History* (Cambridge University Press, 2009). Also J. Edward Chamberlain's *Horse: How the horse has changed civilisation* (Signal Books Ltd, 2006), as well as Stephen Budiansky's seminal text *The Nature of Horses* (The Free Press, 1997).

For more specific information about the horse in war, particularly during World War I, I often turned to Roland Perry's excellent book *The Australian Light Horse* (Hachette, 2015), and Philip Bradley's *Australian Light Horse* (Allen & Unwin, 2016), as well as *Gallipoli to Tripoli* (Browning and Gill, 2012). Paul Daley and Michael Bower's *Armageddon: Two men on an Anzac Trail* (The Miegunyah Press, 2011) is a beautifully curated 'then and now' exploration of the desert campaign during World War I. The letters of Trooper Edward Thompson, in the story 'Ted' (page 101) are completely fictional, though based on real events. I spent a lot of time reading about the Light Horsemen and their mounts while researching my second novel *Only Birds Above*, and I knew that one day I would write about them again.

I doubt there is a single book that has done as much to promote the use of positive reinforcement training as Karen Pryor's *Don't Shoot the Dog* (Bantam Books, 1985) did. Although much has been written since, it is undoubtedly one of the most accessible books ever written about the possibilities of evidence-based training. Jenifer Zelig's *Animal Training 101: The complete and practical guide to the art and science of behaviour modification* (Mill City Press, 2014) is a more thorough examination of all modes of training and is a very useful guide for anyone who works with animals.

The work of B.F. Skinner has forever changed the way we view learning and although much has been written since, I think his works are still of the utmost importance to animal trainers. I doubt they are still in print but it's worth tracking down second-hand copies of *The Behaviour of Organisms* (Appleton-Century-Crofts, 1938) and *Beyond Freedom and Dignity* (Hackett Publishing, 1971). At the same time it is also useful to read Breland and Breland's (1962) paper 'The misbehaviour of organisms' in the journal *American Psychologist* as it illuminates the failure of behaviourists to accommodate their subject's ethology. And it is a fascinating exploration of instinctive drift.

I am happy to admit that some of the things I have learned about horse training I've learned from dog trainers. Dog trainers were amongst the first to embrace evidence-based training and while of course not all the literature is science-based (even if it claims to be) there is a lot of useful knowledge to be gleaned, especially surrounding extinction bursts and variable schedules of reinforcement. Books like Patricia McConnell's *The Other End of the Leash* (Bantam Books, 2002) and Alexandra Horowitz's *Inside of a Dog* (Scribner, 2009) are a great place to begin.

For readers interested in animal consciousness and cognitive abilities I can highly recommend Peter Godfrey-Smith's *Metazoa*

(HarperCollins, 2020) and Marian Stamp Dawkins' *Through Our Eyes Only: The search for animal consciousness* (Oxford University Press, 1993). I can also wholeheartedly recommend Robert Sapolsky's *Junk Food Monkeys* (Headline, 1998), *Why Zebras Don't Get Ulcers* (W.H. Freeman, 1994) and *A Primate's Memoir* (Scribner Book Company, 2002) for anyone with an interest in primate behaviour, stress and the biology of behaviour.

For anything related to biomechanics I always turn to the work of Hilary Clayton. Her books *Conditioning Sport Horses* (Sport Horse Publication, 1991) and *Equine Locomotion* (Saunders Ltd, 2013) co-edited with Willem Beck, are a fantastic reference for anyone interested in how horses move. Equally worthy is Clayton's *The Dynamic Horse* (Sport Horse Publications, 2004).

There are many books about equine behaviour and ethology, and I include some of them here. A.F. Fraser's *The Behaviour of the Horse* (CABI Publishing, 1992), Lucy Rees' *Horses in Company* (J.A. Allen and Co., 2017), Suzanne Rogers' *Equine Behaviour in Mind: Applying behavioural science to the way we keep, work and care for horses* (5M Books Ltd, 2018) and Abigail Hogg's *Horse Behaviour Exposed* (David and Charles, 2009).

I think everyone who is interested in horses and training should, at some stage, read Xenophon's *The Art of Horsemanship* (sometimes called *On Horsemanship* depending on the translation). First published almost 23 centuries ago, Xenophon was a remarkable man who went to war on the back of a horse and yet was still able to appreciate their beauty and advocate for kindness. My copy was published by Dover Publications in 2006.

Martin Seligman's work on learned helplessness is of great importance and I can highly recommend his books *Helplessness: On depression, development and death* (W.H. Freeman and Co. 1975), *Learned Optimism* (Alfred A. Knopf Inc. 1991) and *Flourish* (Atria Books, 2012).

No list of reference material about horse behaviour would be complete without the work of Paul McGreevy. His *Equine Behaviour: A guide for veterinarians and scientists* (Saunders Ltd, 2012) is a wonderful book and I would recommend that anyone who doesn't already own it put it at the top of their Christmas list. Professor McGreevy's *Why Does My Horse?* (Trafalgar, 1996) is still relevant and useful today almost 30 years after publication and should definitely be in the library of every horse lover. Also in the library should be McGreevy's *Carrots and Sticks: Principles of animal training* (Cambridge University Press, 2007) and even – because most horse lovers also love dogs – *A Modern Dog's Life* (UNSW Press, 2009).

Of course, this work would have been impossible without the enormous contribution of Andrew McLean. If there has been a paradigm shift in the way we think and talk about horses in the last two decades it is because he was courageous enough to defend science against centuries of entrenched anthropomorphism. The book that Dr McLean wrote with Paul McGreevy, *Equitation Science* (Wiley-Blackwell, 2010) is absolutely astonishing in its scope and academic rigour. The second edition of *Equitation Science* (Wiley-Blackwell, 2018) was co-authored by Andrew McLean, Paul McGreevy, Janne Winther Christensen and Uta Konig von Borstal and is the best text available for budding equitation scientists and those with an interest in evidence-based training. If you read no other book about horse behaviour this year, make it this one.

I don't think it's exaggerating to say that Andrew McLean's first book, *The Truth About Horses* (Quarto Publishing, 2003) is one of the most important books written about the horse in this century. It is at once both unashamedly evidence-based and yet completely accessible and relevant to people at all stages of their journey with the horse. That it continues to sell well today, more than twenty years after its publication, is testament to its position within the equestrian literary canon. His subsequent books should also be of great interest to anyone interested in evidence-based horse training, in particular *Academic Horse Training* (Australian Equine Behaviour Centre, 2008) and *Modern Horse Training* (Equitation Science International, 2023).

ACKNOWLEDGEMENTS

Writing a book is a team event because without the kindness and support of a great many people this book would never have been more than an idea.

First and foremost my loving thanks go to my family and friends, who not only listened patiently but made time for me so that I could make time for writing. Special thanks to my three beautiful children who have gracefully habituated to an often absent and distracted mother. You make me proud every single day. Clancy, thank you for the illustrations — I hope this is just the first of many mother–daughter creative collaborations.

To my wonderful students, who are always happy to collaborate and experiment. Thank you for sharing your horses, your journeys and your lives with me. Although I'm the one in the middle of the arena I realized long ago that I learn a great deal more than I teach. And for that I am so very grateful.

To the team at Exisle Publishing, in particular Anouska Jones and Karen Gee, thank you for your patience and editing skill.

It's been a pleasure working together to bring an unruly beast of a manuscript to order.

To Jake, thank you for your calm acceptance of the chaos, for your razor-sharp mind, your boundless curiosity and the always interesting conversation. Thank you for believing and supporting and even for the 4.30 alarm.

To Andrew McLean — I have no words to adequately express my gratitude for the part you have played in my life. You have been, and continue to be, the most amazing mentor, teacher and friend. Your academic rigour, generosity, empathy and humanity are a benchmark to which I can only aspire. I am so grateful and so lucky to have you in my life.

INDEX

D

E

F

I

J

K

L

M

N

S